New Wedding Cake Designs

This book is dedicated to my son Benjamin with love.

*When I think of all the friends and family who have touched my life,
I realise that in a world where some have more and some have less
that I am loved and I am blessed.*

Reprinted in 1998
First published in 1997 by Merehurst Limited
Ferry House, 51-57 Lacy Road, Putney, London SW15 1PR
Copyright © 1997 Merehurst Limited
ISBN 1 85391 631 5

A catalogue record for this book is available from the British Library.

Edited by Maureen Callis
Designed by Karen Stafford, DQP
Photography by Alan Marsh
Illustrations by King & King Associates
Colour separation by Chroma Graphics, Singapore
Printed in Singapore by Tien Wah Press

Contents

The heart symbol at the end of each cake description
represents the level of skill required for that decoration.

♥ BEGINNERS

♥ ♥ SOME SKILL REQUIRED

♥ ♥ ♥ MORE ADVANCED

Introduction

The wedding cake is an essential part of the marriage celebrations. While the bride in her dress is the focus of the ceremony, the cake is undoubtedly the centrepiece of the reception.

Like everything in our lives, the style of wedding cakes changes, influenced by fashion, merging cultures and many other factors. The final choice is simply a matter of personal preference.

I find inspiration for my designs in many things that I see around me, from intriguing shapes, interesting textures and bold colour combinations. The idea of striped swags on Summer Days (page 62) came from the interior of marquees often used for summer weddings, and crushed velvet was the inspiration behind Old Time (page 32). Architectural styles, too, can influence — Fantasia (page 112) is reminiscent of the art deco era.

I consider myself incredibly lucky to be able to interpret what I see around me and then express it in my designs. I gain immense satisfaction from passing on my ideas and teaching the skills of sugarcraft.

I hope all cake decorators and sugarcraft devotees will find something to inspire and please them in this book. There is something here for everyone — beginner, expert and brides looking for ideas. I sincerely hope you enjoy the designs in this book — your pleasure will be my reward.

Linda Pawsey

Equipment

BASIC EQUIPMENT

The following is a list of general equipment you will need for creating the cakes in this book.

large and small non-stick rolling pins and boards

tilting turntable

butcher's wrap or non-stick paper

flat and cranked palette knives

small thin blade scissors

plain piping tubes (tips) size 0, 1, 2, 3

parchment piping bags, various sizes

selection of paintbrushes

craft knife

scalpel

scriber

thin wooden or bamboo skewers

soft foam or sponge

ball modelling tools

thin card for templates

squared paper

masking tape

straight edge or icing ruler

tracing paper

perspex or glass

scraper

tweezers

SPECIALIST EQUIPMENT

This is a list of the specialist equipment used in the book.
Details of specific tools or cutters are also given with the relevant cake design.

ring cutters
kit-box templates
lace cutters
assorted stencils
leaf and flower embossers
anglepoise lamp
various leaf and flower cutters
Dresden tool
leaf veiners
quilling cutter
maidenhair fern cutter
rose button mould
clay gun

patchwork cutters
all-in-one rose cutter
silk effect texture tool
plaque cutter
flower former
border mould
straight lace cutter

Templates

The usual way to make templates for side and top designs is to use greaseproof paper or parchment. Calculating the measurements for dividing your cake sides or top into quarters, sixths or whatever division you require is a very tedious and laborious task. Nowadays however help is at hand. Because of the increasing popularity of cake decorating, commercial templates are now available that will do the job for you. These are pre-cut and made of plastic so they can be used time and time again instead of having to start from scratch each time you make a cake. Measurements and guidance for positioning are already marked so your designs can be drawn and marked in a quarter of the time it would normally take.

Basic Recipes and Preparation

Royal icing

2–3 large egg whites
500g (1lb) bridal icing (confectioners') sugar, sifted

1 Ensure all utensils and bowls are clean and free from grease.

2 Crack the egg whites into a bowl and whisk with a fork or whisk, until frothy.

3 Add one third of the icing sugar and mix well.

4 Gradually add the remaining sugar, beating with a fork or whisk after each addition until soft peaks form.

ROYAL ICING *(alternative method)*

*If you prefer to use albumen powder instead of egg whites the proportions
are generally as follows*

12.5g (½ oz or 2–3 teaspoons) albumen powder
90ml (3fl oz) water
500g (1lb) bridal icing (confectioners') sugar, sifted

1 Gently whisk the albumen into the water and leave to stand for 30 minutes.

2 Stir the mixture to dissolve any lumps, then strain. Proceed as above from step 3.

NOTE: If the icing is not beaten enough it will be heavy and glossy.

ROYAL ICING FOR BRUSH EMBROIDERY

4 tablespoons soft peak royal icing
1 teaspoon piping gel

The addition of piping gel to royal icing delays it drying, allowing time to paint and draw the icing to various shapes without it skinning over too quickly. Stir the piping gel gradually into the royal icing.

Sugarpaste and flower paste

I am not including recipes for sugarpaste or flower paste because commercial pastes are now widely available in supermarkets and specialist sugarcraft shops throughout the country. Most are excellent products. I would much rather spend my time on the decoration than the mundane basics and recommend that you do the same!

Unless otherwise specified, all the coloured sugarpaste used throughout the book is the commercial variety.

Flower paste is also sometimes sold as petal paste or gum paste.

Modelling paste

Modelling paste can be made in a variety of ways but I find the easiest is to knead together flower paste and sugarpaste. The ratio depends on the type of decoration you are making.

A 50:50 mixture gives a firm modelling paste suitable for free-standing pieces and cut-out sections that need to be very strong.

For swags and tails a softer mixture of one-third flower paste and two-thirds sugarpaste may be preferred, but please try both ratios as a lot depends on whether you use a firm flower paste or not.

The addition of a pinch of gum tragacanth to the modelling paste immediately before working gives an even stronger end product. This is especially useful for upright decorations that are rolled out very finely. If added to paste for pleating it is essential to work fast once the gum has been added as it starts to thicken very quickly.

Edible glue

Edible glue can now be purchased from most sugarcraft shops but it is quite easy to make your own.

Break 60g (2oz) white sugarpaste or modelling paste into small pieces and place in a heatproof bowl with 2½ tablespoons water. Heat in a microwave or over a saucepan of hot water, stirring until the paste has dissolved. Store in a clean container.

PREPARING THE CAKES

Whether covering a Madeira, sponge or fruit cake the top and sides should be smooth and level. The working surface, rolling pin, knives, etc. should be non-stick, scrupulously clean and dry.

Covering a cake with almond paste

Brush the surface of the cake with apricot glaze.

For a cake that is to have an outer covering of sugarpaste, place the almond paste over the cake in one complete piece and smooth to give rounded edges.

For a cake that is to be royal-iced, cover the top and side(s) separately, taking care to achieve the sharp edge which is synonymous with royal-iced cakes.

NOTE: When working with almond paste never dust the board with cornflour (cornstarch) as particles may become trapped in between the almond paste and sugarpaste or royal icing and cause fermentation.

Morning Glory

Stylish yet incredibly simple to decorate, these cakes are perfect for the beginner or keen amateur who likes to provide the finishing touches for family weddings and other celebrations.

CAKE AND DECORATION MATERIALS

*25cm (10 in), 20cm (8 in) and 15cm (6 in)
teardrop-shaped cakes
apricot glaze
2.5kg (5lb) almond paste
clear alcohol (gin or vodka) for brushing
2kg (4lb) white sugarpaste
30g (1oz) white flower paste
185g (6oz) white modelling paste
edible glue (see page 11)
125g (4oz) royal icing
2.5m x 2.5cm (2 ½ yd x 1 in) white satin ribbon*

EQUIPMENT

*small, medium and large ivy leaf cutters and leaf
veiner
6cm (2½ in) ring cutter
celflaps or plastic wrap
cloud-shaped perspex approx 65cm (25 in) long x
33cm (13 in) at the widest point
Nos.1 and 2 plain piping tubes (tips)
6 wired lily leaves
teardrop-shaped perspex approx 30cm
(12 in) long*

FINISHING TOUCHES

*at least 3 long sprays of good quality silk
variegated ivy
thin white paper ribbon*

⟨⟨ Preparing the cakes ⟩⟩

1 Brush the cakes with apricot glaze and cover with almond paste. Leave to dry. Brush the almond paste with alcohol, cover with white sugarpaste and leave to dry for three days.

⟨⟨ Ivy leaves ⟩⟩

2 Roll out a medium size ball of white flower paste quite thinly and cut a selection of each size of ivy leaf. Soften the edges with a ball tool and leave to dry slightly curved. You will require approximately eighteen of each size leaf.

☙ *Roses* ❧

3 Roll out a large ball of white modelling paste and cut out five 6cm (2½ in) circles. Cover with celflaps or plastic wrap. Take one circle and fold in half. Bring both corners down and into the centre to form a petal shape. Arrange the petals in a circle, overlapping slightly if necessary, and secure with edible glue. Make five more petals and attach inside the first set.

4 Cut three more circles and fold two of them as above. Fold and roll the remaining circle into a tight bud shape, then wrap the two petals around it. Roll to thin the base and remove any surplus paste. Secure this in the centre of the other petals with edible glue.

5 Repeat steps 3 and 4, to make five complete roses.

6 Secure the largest cake to one end of the large piece of perspex with a little royal icing. Attach the white satin ribbon to the base of the cake. Using the No.2 piping tube and royal icing, pipe a snail's trail around the base of the cake.

7 Using the No.1 tube and royal icing, pipe a trailing ivy stem from the centre

of the recess, around the curve of the cake and down onto the perspex. Attach the ivy leaves at intervals along the piped stem, starting with three large leaves in the recess of the cake, medium around the curve, graduating down to the small ones on the perspex. Repeat for the other side.

8 While still reasonably soft, position a rose in the curve of the teardrop so that it fits quite snugly. Secure with royal icing. Fold two lily leaves in half and tuck one in behind each side of the rose.

9 Attach the middle size cake to the other end of the perspex and decorate in the same way (steps 6, 7 and 8).

10 Attach the smallest cake to the teardrop-shaped perspex and decorate as before.

11 Attach a rose to the top of the smallest and largest cake with royal icing.

⚬ *Assembling the cakes* ⚬

12 To display the cakes use small glasses or perspex tubing to raise the large piece of perspex. Position the silk ivy sprays beneath the perspex and twine the white paper ribbon around the edge. Use a straight glass to raise the top tier. Alternatively, drape the ivy around the cakes.

Catherine

This pretty cake with its eye-catching deep pink lace and stringwork would grace any wedding table. The pale pink Cattleya orchids add the finishing touch. I have designed this cake to suit couples who plan to get married abroad and wish to take their own cake with them. The compact spray and stacked cakes enable it to be carried in one box as hand luggage.

CAKE AND DECORATION MATERIALS

23cm (9 in) round cake
15cm (6 in) teardrop-shaped cake
apricot glaze
1.75kg (3½ lb) almond paste
clear alcohol (gin or vodka) for brushing
1.25kg (2½ lb) white sugarpaste
125g (4oz) soft peak royal icing
claret food colouring

EQUIPMENT

30cm (12 in) round cake board
18cm (7 in) teardrop-shaped cake card cut to
exact size of sugarpasted cake
Nos. 0, 1 and 2 plain piping tubes (tips)

FINISHING TOUCHES

3 life-size Cattleya orchids and 3 buds (see page 47)
3 sprays of periwinkle foliage
9 spear-shaped leaves
wired ribbon loops (see page 57)
9 white filler flowers
1m x 1cm (1yd x ½ in) wide pink ribbon

⧼ Preparing the cakes ⧽

1 Brush the cakes with apricot glaze and cover with almond paste. Leave to dry, then brush the almond paste with alcohol. Cover both cakes and the round board only with white sugarpaste. Leave to dry for three days. Attach the cakes to the boards with a little royal icing. Place the small teardrop cake on the top of the round one at the back.

⧼ Making the template ⧽

2 Using the scallop template on page 139 as an approximate guide, draw and cut a length of card, adjusting the size of the scallops to fit the cakes. Holding the card firmly against the base of the round cake, scribe the scallops onto the side. Repeat the scribing on the teardrop cake, positioning the template so that the top of the scallop is on the curve. Leave the shaped area, where the spray sits, plain.

Peach
Celebration

*For the small wedding, this stunning pale peach heart
would grace any celebration table. The floral sprays are
mostly made with silk roses and very simple filler flowers
and leaves, so if you are not a confident flower maker or time
is short, this cake is just for you.*

CAKE AND DECORATION MATERIALS

*25cm (10 in) heart-shaped cake
apricot glaze
1.5kg (3lb) almond paste
clear alcohol (gin or vodka) for brushing
1kg (2lb) pale peach sugarpaste
185g (6oz) pale peach modelling paste
edible glue (see page 11)*

EQUIPMENT

*38cm (15 in) heart-shaped cake board
Kit Box scallop templates
foam pad and thin wooden skewers for pleating
10cm (4 in) ring cutter*

FINISHING TOUCHES

*1m (1yd) pearl beaded trim
10 peach silk roses
15 small peach filler flowers
15 sugar rose leaves
wired ribbon loops (see page 57)
1.5m x 1cm (1½ yd x ½ in) wide pale peach or
cream ribbon
38cm (15 in) heart-shaped board, trimmed with
peach crinkled paper ribbon*

ᕙ Preparing the cake ᕗ

1 Brush the cake with apricot glaze and cover with almond paste. Leave to dry. Brush the almond paste with alcohol, then cover the cake and board with peach sugarpaste. Leave to dry for three days. Attach the cake to the board with a little almond paste mixed with apricot glaze.

2 Measure one side of the cake and determine which Kit Box scallop template will fit four times. Scribe four scallops just below the top edge of the cake on both sides.

ᕙ Swags ᕗ

3 Cut a thin card template 13cm (5 in) square. Roll out the modelling paste as thinly as you can comfortably work with - this will avoid heavy-looking swags. Using the template, cut out a square. Place on the foam and, following the detailed instructions on page 30, form seven pleats. Trim the flat edges off the top and bottom. Gently mould around the ring cutter to form a curve,

↪ *Assembling the cakes* ↩

9 Make up a posy with the daffodils, filler flowers, buds, ribbon loops, tulle and Gypsophilia. Place in the centre of the small cake and attach a tiny strip of pleating around its base.

10 Trim the cake boards with the white ribbon. Stack the cakes traditionally on perspex pillars.

↪ *Almond favours* ↩

Pleated strips have been used to great effect to make an almond favour box. Detailed instructions on how to make this lovely box are on page 93.

Pleating Techniques

Pleated decorations are increasing in popularity. My method for pleating is quick and easy and gives a neat finish. It is a good idea to practise the technique a few times before attempting it on a cake as speed is essential to prevent the pleats cracking.

The paste used for pleating is modelling paste, made by kneading together a mixture of flower paste and sugarpaste (see page 11).

The ratio of flower paste to sugarpaste can be varied considerably and whether you use a firm or soft paste depends on personal choice, but I do not recommend using more than 50% flower paste.

For a firm modelling paste use a half and half mixture. This is better for free-standing pleated sections such as those used on Fantasia (see page 112).

For a softer paste use one third flower paste and two thirds sugarpaste. This mixture is suitable where the pleating is to be attached to the cake top or side.

The elasticity of the modelling paste is important when pleating and the addition of a few drops of glycerine delays the drying time. One or two drops per 30g (1oz) is sufficient.

How to pleat

1 Glue a piece of soft foam or sponge to a cake card. Place the card on a piece of non-slip material. This is important as the pressure needed to pleat the paste will cause the card to slide around.

2 The size of the ball of paste you use will depend on what size decoration you are making. Use card templates for specific shapes, or strips to attach to cake sides. Roll out the paste on a board lightly dusted with a 50:50 mixture of icing (confectioners') sugar and cornflour (cornstarch), and cut to the required size. Transfer the piece to the foam pad.

3 Hold a thin bamboo or wooden skewer in each hand and work from the top of the paste. Press both skewers down firmly into the paste. Slide the bottom skewer up to meet the top one, which should force the paste up in between the skewers and form a pleat. Move the skewers down and repeat until the full section of paste is pleated.

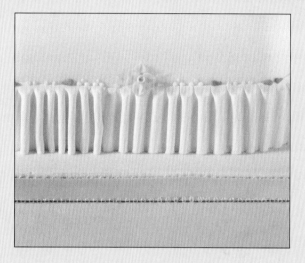

4 The pleated section can now be attached to the cake or set aside to dry, depending on the type of decoration.

Old Time

The unusual draping on these cakes has a look of crushed velvet. Honeysuckle sprays and pressure-piped buds accentuate the flow of the design. The ruched effect is quite simple with a little practice and would be suitable for the enthusiastic beginner to try with care and patience.

CAKE AND DECORATION MATERIALS
*25cm (10 in), 20cm (8 in) and 15cm (6 in)
round cakes
apricot glaze
3kg (6lb) almond paste
2kg (4lb) white sugarpaste
125g (4oz) soft peak royal icing
ivory or cream and spruce green paste colourings
plum, white, cream and chestnut dusting powders
(petal dusts)
30g (1oz) flower paste
375g (12oz) white modelling paste
edible glue (see page 11)*

EQUIPMENT
*33cm (13 in), 28cm (11 in) and 23cm (9 in)
round cake boards
Nos.1 and 2 plain piping tubes (tips)
piece of glass or a cake board
anglepoise lamp
tiny leaf cutter or large drinking straw
Dresden tool or craft knife*

FINISHING TOUCHES
*small, medium, large sprays honeysuckle (page 44)
2m x 1cm (2yd x ½ in) wide white ribbon*

✂ Preparing the cakes ✂

1 Brush the cakes with apricot glaze and cover with almond paste. Leave to dry. Brush the almond paste with alcohol, then cover the cakes and boards with sugarpaste. Leave to dry for three days. Attach the cakes to the boards with a little royal icing. Pipe a snail's trail around the base of the cakes with the No.2 tube.

✂ Honeysuckle ✂

2 Trace the honeysuckle design on page 141 onto paper and place on a piece of glass or a cake board. Cover the design with butcher's wrap or non-stick paper. Smooth out until perfectly flat and secure the edges with masking tape.

3 Add a few drops of water to half of the royal icing until it is softer than soft peak. Colour the icing pale ivory or cream with paste colouring and transfer to a parchment piping bag fitted with the No.1 tube.

Eastern Promise

Strictly for the unconventional. Sumptuous colours together with soft lines and two-colour braid make for an exotic centrepiece. The compact design means these cakes could be taken as hand luggage for a wedding in one of those faraway places that dreams are made of.

CAKE AND DECORATION MATERIALS

25cm (10 in) and 20cm (8 in) round cakes
apricot glaze
2kg (4lb) almond paste
clear alcohol (gin or vodka) for brushing
1.5kg (3lb) beige sugarpaste
60g (2oz) soft peak royal icing
ivory, dark brown, claret and thrift food colourings
piping gel (see page 10)
375g (12oz) beige modelling paste
edible glue (see page 11)

EQUIPMENT

ivy leaf stencil
two No.1 plain piping tubes (tips)
rose button mould

FINISHING TOUCHES

36cm (14 in) heart-shaped cake board covered
with antique gold paper
pink silk peony
1m x 1cm (1yd x ½ in) wide cream ribbon

❀ Preparing the cakes ❀

1 Cut off one quarter of each cake. Brush the cakes with apricot glaze and cover with almond paste. Leave to dry. Brush the almond paste with alcohol, then cover all but the cut edges of the cakes with beige sugarpaste. Do not attach the cakes to the board.

2 Using the ivy leaf stencil and a scriber, mark around the top edge of the cakes, adjusting the position of the stencil so that the leaves fit around the curve. Scribe free-hand stems.

3 Colour the royal icing with ivory and a touch of dark brown food colourings until you achieve a colour slightly darker than the cake. Add the piping gel to half of this icing. Add some claret and a touch of thrift and brown food colourings to the remaining icing to achieve a rich burgundy colour. Fit two parchment piping bags with No.1 tubes and fill one with beige icing and the other with burgundy.

⟲ *Brush embroidery* ⟲

4 Have ready a damp cloth, a small container of water and a sable paint-brush. Working on one side of a leaf at a time, pipe around the scribed outline with the beige icing. Pipe a second line on top of the first. Flatten the tip of the damp paint-brush between finger and thumb and, starting at the top, draw the icing down towards the base of the leaf. Repeat until all the leaves have been piped on both cakes.

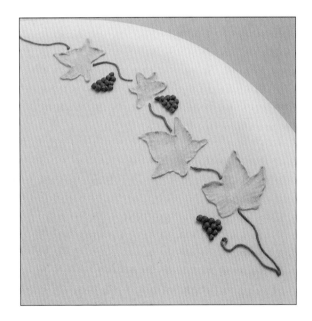

5 Using the burgundy icing, pipe in the stems over the scribed lines. Pipe bulbs of icing formed into triangular shapes to represent bunches of grapes. Be sure the grapes are coloured a deep burgundy as the design is intended to be bold.

⟲ *Assembling the cakes* ⟲

6 When the brush embroidery and piping are thoroughly dry, up-end the cakes and position them offset on the prepared cake board as shown in the main picture, with the small one in front and to the side of the larger one. Attach with a little royal icing.

7 Roll out a golf ball size piece of beige modelling paste and cut out two rose buttons using the mould. Attach one to the top of each cake with edible glue.

8 Add claret and a touch of thrift and dark brown food colourings to half of the remaining beige modelling paste to achieve a dusky pink. Keep both pastes well wrapped to prevent drying out.

9 Roll out a thin strip of beige paste approximately 25cm (10 in) long and 8.5cm (3½ in) wide. Fold under a narrow strip along the long edges to neaten. Repeat with pink paste. Quickly join the two strips together at the top. While still soft, pass one strip over the other to interweave the pieces and make a braid. Attach along the base of the front and sides of the smaller cake with edible glue.

10 Repeat step 9 to make a further two or three pieces. Shorter lengths of paste can be worked if you find braiding difficult. Attach one or two around the sides

and back of the larger cake, and one to sit across the top where the two cakes join.

11 To make the tassel, roll out a small ball of paste in each colour. Cut two strips approximately 10cm (4 in) long by 8.5cm (3½ in) wide and twist together as before (step 9). When twisted, fold the piece up and tuck the ends under to resemble a knot. To make the fringe, roll out a small ball of paste in each colour and cut each into a strip 10cm (4 in) long and 5cm (2 in) wide. Using a craft knife, cut into the strips two-thirds of the way across. Glue one on top of the other and roll up as shown. Secure to the underside of the knot.

12 Attach the tassel to the braid in front of the smaller cake. Attach the silk peony in the recess between the cakes and trim the cake board with the cream ribbon.

Pastel Magic

*Petal shapes are always popular for wedding cakes.
This one is enhanced by the patchwork side design
and beautiful cake top ornament. This is made
from modelling paste and decorated with the
same rose design.*

CAKE AND DECORATION MATERIALS
*25cm (10 in), 20cm (8 in) and 15cm (6 in)
petal-shaped cakes
apricot glaze
3kg (6lb) almond paste
clear alcohol (gin or vodka) for brushing
2.5kg (5lb) white sugarpaste
60g (2oz) soft peak royal icing
white vegetable fat (shortening)
250g (8oz) white modelling paste
small ball of leaf-coloured flower paste
gold and peach dusting powders (petal dusts)
peach and leaf green food colourings
16 small peach silk or sugar roses*

EQUIPMENT
*33cm (13 in), 28cm (11 in) and 23cm (9 in)
petal-shaped cake boards
set of three rose design patchwork cutters
No.1 plain piping tube (tip)
tiny leaf and quilling cutters
Dresden tool or small leaf veiner*

FINISHING TOUCHES
*cake top ornament (see page 116)
2m x 1cm (2yd x ½ in) wide white ribbon*

Preparing the cakes

1 Brush the cakes with apricot glaze and cover with almond paste. Leave to dry. Brush the almond paste with alcohol, then cover the cakes and boards with white sugarpaste. Leave to dry for three days. Attach the cakes to the boards with a little royal icing.

Patchwork roses

2 Lightly grease a non-stick board with white vegetable fat. Roll out a walnut size piece of white modelling paste quite thinly. Lightly grease the cutting edge of the largest patchwork cutter to prevent sticking and press firmly onto the paste. Remove the cutter — the rose should stay on the board. Remove any surplus surrounding paste with tweezers and trim the edges with a craft knife if necessary. Leave for a few minutes to skin over, then attach to the largest cake in the centre of a scalloped side. Cut a further piece but remove the sides to leave only the centre rose. When partially dry, attach this to

the first rose. Repeat five more times to complete the bottom tier.

3 Repeat step 2 with the medium cutter for the middle tier and the smallest cutter for the top tier.

4 Using soft peak royal icing and the No.1 tube, pipe a small snail's trail around the base of all three cakes.

∽ *Leaves* ∽

5 Roll out the green flower paste very thinly and cut several tiny leaves. Mark a centre vein with the Dresden tool or small veiner. Ball the edges to give movement. You will require thirty-six leaves for the cakes and up to six for the top ornament.

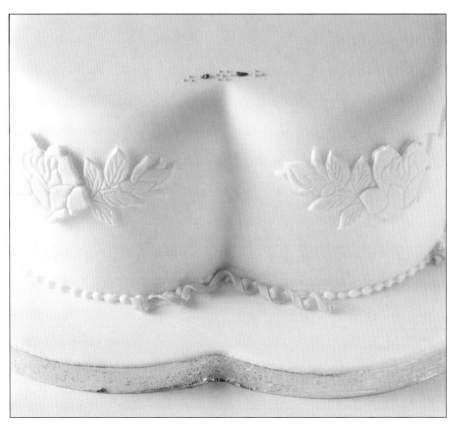

∞ *Ribbon curls* ∞

6 Roll out a small quantity of white modelling paste quite thinly. Using the quilling cutter, roll and cut several strips. Dust with a mixture of gold and peach dusting powders and cut as follows: for the large cake cut three 13cm (5 in) strips and wrap around a bamboo skewer to curl; for the middle cake cut and curl three 10cm (4 in) strips; for the small cake cut and curl three 7.5cm (3 in) strips. Leave for a few minutes to dry a little, then remove the skewers.

7 Centre a ribbon curl in the scallop recesses at the base of each cake. Using No. 1 tubes and peach and green icing, pipe a tiny leaf and flower detail at the top edge of each scallop (see bottom picture on facing page).

8 Using royal icing, attach a small peach rose to the centre of each ribbon curl and two leaves on either side.

∞ *Assembling the cakes* ∞

9 Position the cake top ornament on the top tier. Trim the cake boards with the white ribbon. Arrange the cakes offset on perspex, or set upright in the traditional way using pillars.

> *TIP*
> *Practise new techniques several times before attempting to execute them on a special cake. Obviously the more you practise the neater your results will be.*

Flowers for all Seasons

Flowers add a seasonal touch and a splash of colour to any cake. They may be silk or sugar, depending on preference and, of course, skill and time. The quality of silk flowers has improved tremendously over the years and I would have no hesitation in using them.

When reproducing flowers in sugar, it is a good idea to have a real specimen or a good photograph to work from. Whether you aim for botanical accuracy is entirely a matter of personal preference and time available. But it's worth remembering that the recipients of the cake will not view your work with the critical eye that you do — on the contrary, they will no doubt be delighted to have such a wonderful masterpiece to grace their wedding or family gathering.

Flower making has been popular for many years and there are some excellent books available that will help you. This book deals mainly with cake designs and decorations, but flowers frequently play an important part. I am therefore including brief details for making some of the flowers used in this book. Templates are shown on page 135 and 26-gauge wires have been used unless otherwise stated.

Honeysuckle

1 To make the buds, roll a pea size piece of cream-coloured flower paste into a long cone. Insert a wire into the narrow end

and bend the rounded top slightly. Tape together five or more buds. Make small green buds in the same way.

2 To make the flower, tape five tiny brown stamen to a wire. Make a slightly larger cone than before and insert a celpin or skewer into the fat end. Using small thin blade scissors, make two cuts in the paste to form one thin petal. Cut small V shapes from either side of the petal. Now thin the paste and make three tiny cuts in the end of the large section to form four small petals.

3 Leave to dry, then brush the buds and the outside of the flowers with plum dusting powder (petal dust) to which a tiny amount of brown has been added.

4 Use a medium size plain leaf cutter and green flower paste for the leaves.

5 See picture for guidance for arrangement of buds and leaves.

Lily

1 To make the stigma, roll a small ball of white flower paste onto a wire to form a long thin cone. Using cranked tweezers, pinch the top end of the paste into three equal sections. Leave to dry, then brush the whole length of the stigma with pale green dusting powder (petal dust) and the tip brown. Tape six lily stamen around this centre.

2 To make the inner petals, roll out a thin sausage of paste. Flatten and roll either side until a thin ridge is left up the middle. Using a cutter or template, cut a petal with the ridge centred. Vein and ball the petal and mark a groove along the length of the ridge. Insert a white wire into the base and leave to dry over a curved former. Repeat to make two more. Colour with dusting powder.

3 To make the outer petals, repeat as above but without the ridge.

4 Tape the inner petals around the stamen and stigma, then position the outer petals on the outside in between the inner petals.

Alstroemeria

(PERUVIAN LILY)

1 To make the stigma, flatten and cut the end of a stamen thread into strips and attach to a wire. Tape five green headed stamen around the stigma.

2 To make the outer petals, roll out a medium size ball of white flower paste, leaving one edge slightly thicker. Place the base of a petal cutter or template against this thicker edge and cut out three petals. Vein and ball the petals, insert a wire and leave to dry over a curved former.

3 Repeat to cut and form three inner petals. Using a picture for reference, mark and colour with dusting powder (petal dust).

Singapore Orchid

1 To make the column, form a tiny piece of white flower paste into a tapered cone about 1cm (½ in) long. Insert a 28-gauge wire into the thin end. Snip the other end to divide the tip into three. Flatten the outer cut sections. Set aside to dry.

2 Roll out a small ball of white flower paste and cut a tongue (see page 135 for template). Ball and frill the curved edges. Brush a little edible glue (see page 11) on the pointed end and wrap it around the column.

3 Roll out and cut back the three-petal section and the two side petals. Ball and frill all the edges. Referring again to the template or a picture, glue the side petals onto the three-petal section and fold it around the tongue and column.

4 To make buds, form a small piece of paste into a cone and pinch one side of the thicker end. Gently curve the fine tip to one side. Insert a 28-gauge wire into the thicker base. Leave to dry.

Miniature Iris

1 Roll a small ball of purple flower paste onto a wire to form a small cone. Leave to dry. Using a three-petal freesia cutter or template and rolled-out flower paste, cut out two sets of petals. Ball and vein. Glue the centre of each piece and thread onto the wired cone. Curve the first set forward and the second set backward. Set aside to dry thoroughly.

Cattleya Orchid

1 To make the column, roll a small ball of paste onto a slightly curved white wire and form a long cone. Cut into the paste at the fatter end of the cone on either side of the wire. This effectively divides the fat tip into three sections. Flatten the small outer sections between finger and thumb and gently bend in towards the centre. Leave to dry.

2 Roll out a medium size ball of paste, leaving one edge slightly thicker. Cut three sepals, positioning the base of the template or cutter on the thicker edge of the paste. Vein and ball, insert a wire then leave to dry over a curved former. Using a petal cutter or template, cut two petals. Vein, ball and dry as above.

3 Cut a tongue from white paste and frill the edge. Glue the top and wrap around the dried column. Using a picture or specimen for reference, colour with dusting powder (petal dust).

NOTE: On all cakes where wired flowers are used a flower pick must be inserted into the cake to hold the wires. Remove the pick and wired flowers before serving.

Eve

*The opulence of gold and white — just the right combination
on a single tier for a small but stylish wedding. The delicate
one-step collars are easier to make than they look.*

CAKE AND DECORATION MATERIALS

*25cm (10 in) hexagonal cake
apricot glaze
2kg (4lb) almond paste
1kg (2lb) soft peak royal icing
1m x 2.5cm (1yd x 1 in) wide gold ribbon
albumen powder
30g (1oz) white modelling paste*

EQUIPMENT

*33cm (13 in) hexagonal gold cake board
Nos.0, 1, 2 and 3 plain piping tubes (tips)
3 pieces of glass or perspex approx 15cm (6 in)
square for drying run-outs
anglepoise lamp
7.5cm (3 in) oval cutter*

FINISHING TOUCHES

*6 unwired small double blossoms
12 wired small double blossoms and buds
6 small leaves (any variety will do)
3 wired gold ribbon loops (see page 57)*

Preparing the cake

1 Brush the cake with apricot glaze and cover with almond paste. Attach to the cake board and coat with royal icing. Set aside to dry.

2 Attach the ribbon around the base of the cake with royal icing, then pipe a snail's trail on the board around the ribbon with the No. 1 tube.

Side design

3 Fit a parchment piping bag with the No.2 tube and half fill with soft peak royal icing. Starting at the centre of one side

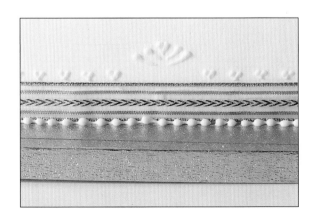

and 2.5cm (1 in) above the ribbon, form a small heart by piping two bulbs of icing side by side with the tails tapering in at the base. Pipe two further bulbs on either side, curving the ends in and under the heart as shown. Pipe five small hearts just above the ribbon on either side of the centre design.

4 At a point 2.5cm (1 in) down from the top edge of the cake, pipe the same design upside down to mirror the first. If necessary use a 2.5cm (1 in) strip of paper attached to the top edge for guidance.

∽ *One-step collars* ∽

5 Trace the collar design on page 138 onto two pieces of white paper. Place the design on a piece of perspex or glass and cover with butcher's wrap or non-stick paper. Smooth out until perfectly flat and secure with masking tape.

6 Thin some royal icing with albumen, adding the liquid a little at a time until you have the right consistency (see Note). Keep the bowl covered with a damp cloth.

7 Fit a piping bag with the No.3 tube and half fill with the royal icing. Carefully pipe around the traced outline, allowing the icing to flow and form. The amount of pressure you use will determine the width of the lines. With practice you can alter the

thickness of the piping to give variety to the design. Dry under the lamp to give a sheen to the surface.

8 Repeat step 7 to make seven further collar sections (this includes two spares).

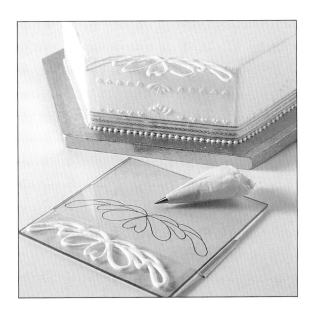

∽ *Assembling the cake* ∽

9 Attach the dried collar sections to the top edges of the cake with royal icing. Using a No.0 or 1 tube pipe small hearts and lines following the contour of the collars. Attach an unwired small double blossom at the corners of the cake between the collar sections.

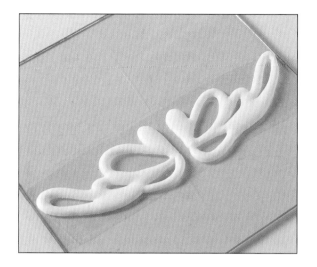

small ball of modelling paste. Set the arrangement onto the oval of paste and attach the dried run-outs to the back with royal icing. Secure to the centre of the cake with royal icing.

10 To make the cake top ornament, pipe two sections and a spare as in step 7, using a half section only of the collar design.

11 Cut an oval of modelling paste and leave to dry.

12 Arrange approximately twelve wired small double blossoms and buds, six leaves and three wired gold ribbon loops in a

Rosebud

Delicate coloured piping and extension work complement the rosebud sprays and striking stencilled side decoration.

CAKE AND DECORATION MATERIALS
*25 x 20cm (10 x 8 in), 20 x 15cm (8 x 6 in) and 15 x 10cm (6 x 4 in) oval cakes
apricot glaze
2.75kg (5½lb) almond paste
clear alcohol (gin or vodka) for brushing
2kg (4lb) cream sugarpaste
125g (4oz) soft peak royal icing
tiny amount each of white petal cream and white vegetable fat (shortening)
spruce green and claret paste colourings
60g (2oz) cream modelling paste*

EQUIPMENT
*33 x 28cm (13 x 11 in), 28 x 23cm (11 x 9 in) and 23 x 18cm (9 x 7 in) oval cake boards
rose embosser
miniature wreath stencil (rose design)*

FINISHING TOUCHES
*pale pink roses and buds
white blossoms and buds
various foliage and miniature Gypsophilia
wired ribbon loops (see page 57)
2m x 1cm (2yd x ½ in) wide pink ribbon and
1m x 1cm (1yd x ½ in) wide white ribbon*

Preparing the cakes

1 Brush the cakes with apricot glaze and cover with almond paste. Leave to dry. Brush the almond paste with alcohol, then cover the cakes and boards with cream sugarpaste. Emboss the sugarpaste on the edge of the boards. Leave to dry for three days. Attach the cakes to the boards with a little royal icing.

2 Measure the circumference of each cake and lightly mark the centre front, back and sides at the base.

3 Trace the templates on page 139 and scribe onto the sides of the cakes, using the centre side mark to position.

Rose stencil

4 Mix together the white petal cream and white vegetable fat on a scraper. Add a small amount of spruce green paste colouring to produce a pale shade of green. Repeat with claret food colouring to form a pale pink.

5 Press a small piece of modelling paste onto the stencil firmly enough for the raised design to show through the cut-out sections.

6 Turn over the modelling paste with the stencil still attached and, using a small piece of sponge dipped in the green, dab lightly to colour the leaf sections. Using a clean piece of sponge and the pale pink, colour the rose cut-outs. Carefully remove the stencil and cut out the wreath shape with a craft knife or scalpel. Place on a piece of foam and leave to dry.

7 Repeat steps 5 and 6 to colour and cut a further five wreaths, two for each cake. When dry, attach one to the front and one to the back of each cake.

8 Using a No.2 piping tube (tip) and soft peak royal icing, pipe a snail's trail around the base of each cake.

∽ *Bridge work* ∾

9 Using a No.1 tube and soft peak royal icing begin piping the bridge work. Support the cake so that you can work at eye level if possible. Work the sides of each cake until each scallop has its first base line. Leave to dry. Pipe a second line on top of the

first, using a fine damp paintbrush to guide any loose ends into place. Clean the tube before commencing each new line to prevent bulbs forming. The bridge work should consist of seven lines. Leave to dry completely.

10 Using the No.1 tube, pipe a small pink and green flower and leaf design above the scallops. This will show through the completed extension work.

∽ *Extension work* ∾

11 Commence piping lines which extend from the scribed top line of the design down and away to the outer edge of the

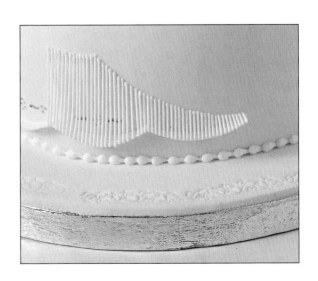

bridge work. Pipe the lines as close together as you can — the gap between each line should be the same width as the width of the piped extension work. Work on a small section directly in front of you to ensure your lines are absolutely straight.

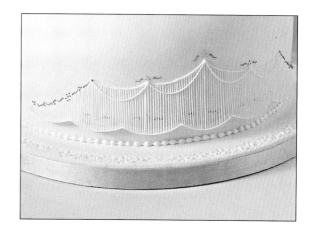

12 When you have completed the extension work on all the cakes, finish off the bottom edge by piping an additional scalloped line over the top of the extension work. Pipe over the top edge of the middle scallops and pipe a second scallop slightly below, resting on the extension work. Repeat the coloured flower and leaf design on the outer edges of the extension work and above the highest points of the scallops.

of the top tier and attach more flowers, leaves and ribbon loops at the base. Attach the sprays to the centre of the other two tiers. Trim the large and small cake boards with the pink ribbon and the middle board with the white ribbon. Arrange the cakes offset on perspex stands.

∽ *Assembling the cakes* ∽

13 Wire together a mixture of roses, buds, blossoms, foliage, Gypsophilia and wired ribbon loops to make two sprays for the larger cakes. For the top tier make two small mixed sprays, secure to a piece of modelling paste and curve in at the top to make a horseshoe shape. Attach to the centre

TIP
Use run-out consistency royal icing to coat the bridgework for extra strength and a fine brush to spread the icing.

Using Ribbons

*R*ibbons are a very useful addition to any floral arrangement —
they can be used to add colour and give definition and shape.
But don't use too many or they will overwhelm the arrangement.
Ribbons should be used to complement the flowers, so add them with
discretion. There is now a fantastic selection available from cake
decoration equipment shops and florist suppliers.

Certain things need to be considered when
deciding on the colours of ribbon to use in
your arrangements and floral decorations.

Ribbon loops that match the colour of the
flowers and foliage used in your sprays will
make a subtle addition that is hardly
noticeable but nevertheless effective. Rosebud (page 52) is a good example: here soft

pink, pale green and cream have been used
to enhance the delicate overall effect.

If you require something more striking,
this can be achieved in one or two ways.
You can simply add very brightly coloured
ribbon loops. These could be the same
colour as the bridesmaids' dresses or
contrast with the flowers in the sprays.
Alternatively, you can pick out a strong
colour from the flowers. In Summer Days
(page 62) I have picked out the deep red
markings on the Alstroemeria. If all the
flowers were the same dark red this colour
might be a little too much, but using
ribbon to enhance a little dark or unusual
colour is usually very effective. This is a
good way to deal with an often difficult
problem.

I have used mostly muted colours on the
designs in this book as I feel the flowers
should be the focal point.

There are many different ways to wire ribbons, in single loops, twos or threes. Alternatively single strips of ribbon can form long or short tails.

When using tulle or organza ribbons I frequently cut them into smaller loops after they have been wired (see picture below). In most arrangements use 28-gauge wire for ribbon loops, as anything finer will not stay in position in the arrangement.

I use the figure of eight bow more than any other as it looks good in most arrangements.

Figure of eight bow

Fold the ribbon until the loops are the required size and in a figure of eight with a tail. You should have three layers between your finger and thumb. Cut the ribbon from the roll. Pinch the centre of the loops together and twist a hooked wire firmly around the centre. Pull the loops into shape and tape the base to ensure they stay in position.

Ribbon trims

A simple ribbon around the side of a cake can make all the difference to the finished effect. A plain coloured ribbon that tones with or complements colours used in the decoration is usually quite sufficient.

For more impact, use a broader patterned ribbon. If time and skill allow, copy the ribbon design onto the cake in piped decorations and line work.

Another pleasing effect can be achieved by using tulle or organza ribbons, which give a light delicate touch and allow the colour of the cake to show through.

Chloe

Yellow and white make a pleasant change from the more traditional white wedding cake. The lily theme is reflected in the royal icing run-outs.

CAKE AND DECORATION MATERIALS

250g (8oz) white sugarpaste
25cm (10 in) round cake
20 x 15cm (8 x 6 in) oval cake
apricot glaze
2.5kg (5lb) almond paste
clear alcohol (gin or vodka) for brushing
2kg (4lb) sugarpaste, coloured yellow with melon yellow paste colouring
125g (4oz) soft peak royal icing
125g (4oz) modelling paste, coloured as above
albumen powder (optional)

EQUIPMENT

33cm (13 in) round cake board
28 x 23cm (11 x 9 in) oval cake board
squared paper
glass-headed pin
Nos. 0 and 1 plain piping tubes (tips)
anglepoise lamp

FINISHING TOUCHES

4 lilies and 4 buds (see page 45)
4 lily leaves
2 sprays of larkspur
wired ribbon loops and organza bows (see page 57)
2m x 1cm (2yd x ½ in) wide lemon ribbon

ᨠ Preparing the cakes ᨠ

1 Cover the cake boards with white sugarpaste and set aside to dry. Brush the cakes with apricot glaze and cover with almond paste. Leave to dry. Brush the almond paste with alcohol, then cover the cakes with yellow sugarpaste. Leave to dry for three days. Attach the cakes to the boards with a little royal icing.

2 Using squared paper and a glass-headed pin, prick through the paper onto the surface of the cakes and onto the boards to mark squares approximately 2.5cm (1 in) in size.

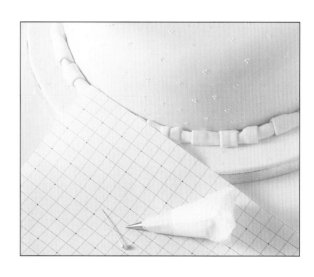

3 Using soft peak royal icing and the No.0 tube, pipe clusters of three tiny dots, making sure one dot covers the pin prick. Pipe white dots on the yellow cakes and yellow dots on the white cake boards (see picture on page 58).

4 Roll out about 30g (1oz) yellow modelling paste and cut a strip 2.5 to 5cm (1 to 2 in) wide. Slide a bamboo skewer under one end of the strip of paste and lift a small section. Holding the paste, press the skewer down onto the centre of the raised section to form two folds. Repeat the procedure down the length of the paste, leaving small, uneven gaps between the folds.

5 Fold the paste in half widthways and press the long edges lightly together. Press the folded side of the paste against an icing ruler to lift. Attach to the cake board with the flat edge tucked against the base of the cake.

6 Repeat steps 4 and 5. To join sections leave one end open and fold the edges under. Pinch the end of the section to be attached, form into a point and slot into the open end of the first section. Edge both cakes in this way.

∽ *Lily run-outs* ∽

7 Trace the two lily templates on page 138 onto two separate pieces of paper. Place on a piece of perspex or glass and cover with butcher's wrap or non-stick paper. Smooth out until perfectly flat and secure with masking tape. Using soft peak royal icing and the No.1 tube, pipe the outline of the designs.

8 Thin some royal icing with water or albumen (see Note). Half-fill a medium piping bag with the run-out icing (no tube is required). Snip off the end of the bag (to the size of a No.2 tube) and squeeze the icing into another bag. This is a good way to get rid of air bubbles. (You will be able to hear them popping!)

9 Cut the same amount off this bag and flood the lilies. Work on alternate petals so that they can skin over without running into each other. Dry under the lamp to obtain a sheen. Leave to dry completely, then carefully remove from the paper and attach to the cakes with a little royal icing.

∽ *Assembling the cakes* ∾

10 Wire the lilies, leaves, larkspur and wired ribbon loops together to make two similar sprays. Secure them to a piece of modelling paste directly on the large cake board, with one spray standing up behind the other, as shown. Attach wired organza bows to hide the paste and cover the base of the sprays. Trim both boards with the lemon ribbon. Present the cakes as shown, slightly offset on a perspex stand.

NOTE
I recommend using albumen as it gives a stronger run-out. Dissolve 1 tablespoon albumen powder in 75ml (2½fl oz) water.
Stir the liquid into the royal icing a little at a time until you have the right consistency. To assess how much liquid is required, draw a spoon across the icing and count slowly to 10 — the icing should then have levelled out and show no mark of the spoon.
Keep the bowl covered with a damp cloth.

Summer Days

The striped 'marquee' swags in this design are achieved with a very fine stencil. I have used yellow Alstroemeria in the sprays, but lilies or other summer flowers of a similar size and colour would be suitable.

CAKE AND DECORATION MATERIALS

*28cm (11 in), 23cm (9 in) and 18cm (7 in)
hexagonal cakes
apricot glaze
4kg (8lb) almond paste
clear alcohol (gin or vodka) for brushing
3kg (6lb) white sugarpaste
60g (2oz) soft peak royal icing
edible glue (see page 11)
little white vegetable fat (shortening)
60g (2oz) white flower paste
melon yellow paste colouring
superwhite dusting powder (petal dust)
500g (1lb) white modelling paste*

EQUIPMENT

*36cm (14 in), 30cm (12 in) and 25cm (10 in)
hexagonal cake boards
No.2 plain piping tube (tip)
lace cutter and narrow striped stencil*

FINISHING TOUCHES

*2m x 2.5mm (2yd x ⅛ in) wide yellow ribbon
Alstroemeria flowers and 9 buds (see page 46)
12 medium white filler flowers and 9 white buds
7 sprays of ivy and green Gypsophilia
wired ribbon loops (see page 57)
3m x 1cm (3yd x ½ in) wide white ribbon*

∽ Preparing the cakes ∽

1 Brush the cakes with apricot glaze and cover with almond paste. Leave to dry. Brush the almond paste with alcohol, then cover the cakes and boards with white sugarpaste. Leave to dry for three days. Attach the cakes to the boards with a little royal icing.

2 Measure the depth of the cakes, then scribe a line around the cakes a little lower than half the depth. Attach the yellow ribbon with a small line of royal icing or edible glue. Pipe a snail's trail around the base of the cakes with the royal icing and the No.2 tube.

∽ Lace ∽

3 Lightly grease a non-stick board with white vegetable fat. Roll out a small ball of white flower paste very thinly and cut a minimum of forty lace pieces with the lace cutter, retaining the centres. Place on a piece of sponge or foam to dry, then attach to the centre of the cake sides and the board as shown (see pictures on page 64).

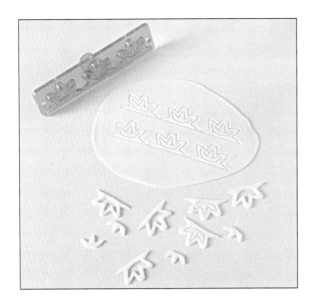

an airbrush. Fold over the top and bottom edges of the paste and press lightly. Place a skewer underneath the strip and raise up the paste in the middle. Pinch lightly to allow the paste to meet underneath the skewer, then remove it. Now press the skewer down directly onto the centre of the top of the raised section. This should form two pleats. Press the pleats firmly at each end up towards the top of the swag so that they almost merge together at both ends. Repeat to make and attach seventeen further swags, ensuring that each swag has the same number of pleats.

7 Attach the swags to the top of the cakes across the corners so that the joins are in the centre of the sides above the lace. Trim if necessary.

✌ Bows ✌

8 Roll out and cut a strip of modelling paste 13cm (5 in) long and 2.5cm (1 in) wide. Fold the ends into the middle, then pinch and glue them together to make the bow. Cut another strip 10cm (4 in) long and

✌ Swags ✌

4 Make a thin card template 2.5cm (1in) wider than one side of the hexagon and approximately 7.5cm (3 in) deep.

5 Mix some melon yellow paste colouring with a small quantity of white vegetable fat. Add some superwhite dusting powder to lighten if required. (If you do lighten the colour, ensure that you mix enough to complete the swags for all the cakes.)

6 Roll out a golf ball size piece of white modelling paste and cut out a rectangle, using the template as a pattern. Lay the stencil over the paste, hold firmly, and brush or sponge on the prepared yellow colouring until all the stripes are marked. Alternatively, use

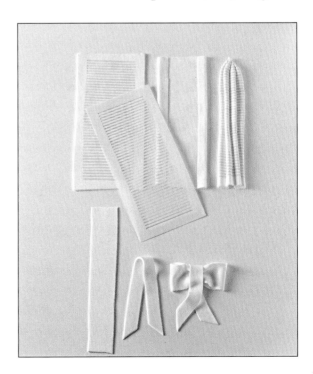

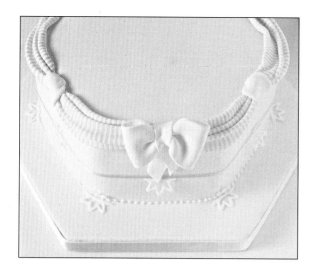

using an extra foliage spray for the top tier. Add wired ribbon loops as desired.

10 Attach the larger spray to the centre of the top tier, and the others halfway along one side of the remaining tiers.

11 Trim the cake boards with the white ribbon. These cakes can be stacked one on top of the other using pillars or offset as shown, using a perspex or chrome stand.

1cm (½ in) wide. Lay the bow in the centre of this strip. Fold the strip over the top to form the tail. Repeat to make eight further bows. While still soft, attach the bows at the point where the swags join on alternate sides of the cakes. Attach further folded strips 5cm (2 in) long and 2.5cm (1 in) wide over the remaining joins.

∽ *Assembling the cakes* ∽

9 Divide the flowers and foliage equally and wire together to make three sprays,

NOTE
Ensure that the swags are draped neatly and all meet at the centre point on the sides of the cakes, and that the bottom edge rests on the cake in the same position for each swag. Follow the instructions for Peach Celebration (page 22) if you feel you need a template for help with positioning the swags.

Rebekah

For an English rose, pretty heart-shaped cakes.
The delicate patchwork collars are deceptively easy to
make so this cake is suitable for those who prefer
royal icing but are not experts.

CAKE AND DECORATION MATERIALS
25cm (10 in) and 20cm (8 in) heart-shaped
cakes
apricot glaze
1.75kg (3½lb) almond paste
1.5kg (3lb) soft peak royal icing
1.5m x 5cm (1½yd x 2 in) wide pink and white
rose patterned ribbon
pinch of gum tragacanth
125g (4oz) white modelling paste
little white vegetable fat (shortening) for greasing
30g (1oz) pale pink modelling paste
15g (½oz) white flower paste
edible glue (see page 11)

EQUIPMENT
33cm (13 in) and 28cm (11 in) heart-shaped
cake boards
Nos.0, 1 and 2 plain piping tubes (tips)
three sizes hearts-and-flowers patchwork cutters
tweezers
heart-shaped template (see Note)
5cm (2 in) all-in-one rose cutter
petal veiner
flower former

∞ *Preparing the cakes* ∞

1 Brush the cakes with apricot glaze and cover with almond paste. Attach to the cake boards and coat with royal icing. Set aside to dry.

2 Attach the ribbon around the middle of the cake sides with royal icing.

∞ *Side design* ∞

3 Using a No.0 or No.1 tube (depending on which you feel more confident using) and royal icing, pipe curved lines and leaves

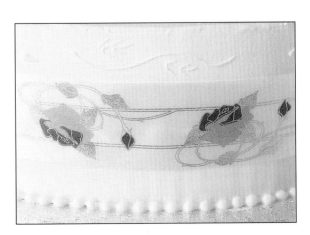

above the ribbon around the sides of the cakes, using the diagram on page 141 as a guide.

4 Following the second stage diagram, complete the piping above the ribbon and pipe a similar design below.

∽ *Patchwork collars* ∾

5 Knead a pinch of gum tragacanth into the white modelling paste.

6 Lightly grease a non-stick board with white vegetable fat and roll out a medium size ball of paste quite thinly. Lightly grease the cutting edge of the largest patchwork cutter and press firmly onto the paste. When the cutter is removed the paste should stay on the board. Remove the surplus paste with tweezers and trim the edges with a craft knife if necessary. Lift carefully and leave to dry thoroughly on foam. Cut a further two pieces using the large cutter.

(two intertwined hearts) only. Cut eight pairs of hearts and one single heart. Set aside to dry on foam.

9 Place the heart-shaped template in the centre of the large cake. Using a No.0 or No.1 tube and royal icing, pipe tiny dots around the heart, then position and attach the single pink heart at the top. Repeat on the small cake, omitting the pink heart.

7 Repeat step 6 using the medium size cutter.

8 Repeat step 5 and preparation stage of step 6 with pink modelling paste and the smallest cutter. Cut out the middle section

10 Study the main picture to establish the positioning of the dried patchwork collars and hearts. Attach three large collars and four intertwined hearts to the large cake. Attach the smaller collars and remaining hearts to the small cake.

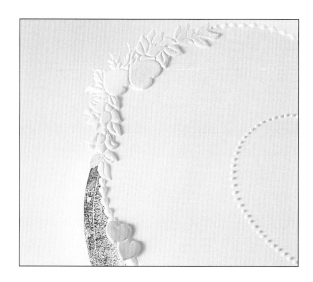

11 Using the No.2 tube and royal icing, pipe a snail's trail around the top edge of both cakes in between the collars and hearts, and around the base of the cakes.

∽ *Cake top decoration* ∾

12 Roll out a medium size ball of white flower paste and cut three flowers with the rose cutter. Vein the petals and ball around the edges to thin and frill. Attach the flowers one on top of the other with edible glue in the flower former. Set aside to dry. Add stamen to the rose if you wish (see page 100).

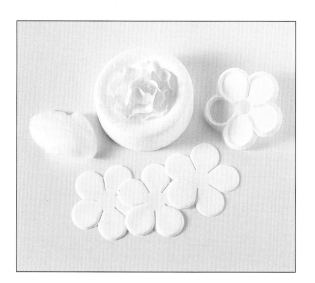

13 Roll out a small ball of pink modelling paste and cut four strips 10 x 1cm (4 x ½ in). Fold each in half to form loops. Roll out and cut two further strips 15 x 1cm (6 x ½ in) and cut inverted V shapes out of the ends.

∽ *Assembling the cakes* ∾

14 Arrange the ribbons and tails as shown below inside the piped heart on the small cake and attach the rose to the centre with royal icing.

15 These cakes are best presented offset. If you wish to stack them, omit the piped heart from the bottom tier or reduce it in size so that it fits inside the pillars.

NOTE
I used a bought heart-shaped template, but if you prefer to make your own, see page 141.

Hearts and Bows

*The stylish bows and eye-catching
board texture are complemented by pressure-piped lace
on this lovely heart-shaped wedding cake.*

CAKE AND DECORATION MATERIALS
*25cm (10 in), 20cm (8 in) and 15cm (6 in) heart-
shaped cakes
apricot glaze
3.5kg (7lb) almond paste
clear alcohol (gin or vodka) for brushing
2.5kg (5lb) white sugarpaste
125g (4oz) soft peak royal icing
lilac food colouring and dusting powder (petal dust)
185g (6oz) white modelling paste
edible glue (see page 11)*

EQUIPMENT
*33cm (13 in), 28cm (11 in) and 23cm (9 in)
heart-shaped cake boards
silk-effect texture tool
greaseproof (parchment) paper
Nos. 2, 1 and 0 plain piping tubes (tips)
kit box heart-shaped templates
1cm (½ in) squared paper*

FINISHING TOUCHES
*6 miniature iris and 12 buds (see page 47)
white blossoms and buds
6 sprays of any small leaves
3m x 1cm (3yd x ½ in) wide pale lilac ribbon*

∽ Preparing the cakes ∽

1 Brush the cakes with apricot glaze and cover with almond paste. Leave to dry. Brush the almond paste with alcohol, then cover the cakes and boards with sugarpaste. Mark around the edges of the boards with the texture tool. Leave to dry for three days. Attach the cakes to the boards with a little royal icing.

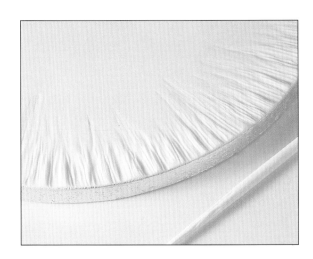

2 Using greaseproof paper, make templates the depth and half the circumference of each cake. Draw two sweeping curves, starting halfway along one side and making one curve lower than the

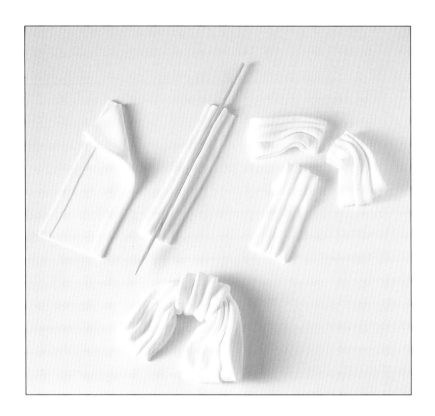

other (see main picture). Hold the template against the side of the cake and scribe the curves onto the sugarpaste. Reverse the template and repeat on the other side of the cake. Repeat for each cake.

3 Using the No.2 piping tube and white royal icing, pipe small shells around the base of each cake. Colour a small quantity of royal icing lilac and pipe three small dots with the No.0 tube on the board in front of every third shell. Repeat on all three cakes.

∞ *Bows* ∞

4 Cut a thin card template 13 x 7.5cm (5 x 3 in). Roll out a medium size ball of white modelling paste quite thinly and, pressing lightly to hold the template in position, cut around it. This section will form one half of the bow. Fold over both long sides. Using a bamboo skewer, lift up the section lengthways in the middle and press to form a tuck. Fold the piece in half to form a loop. Repeat to make five more loops.

5 Using the same template, cut and form three more pleated sections, but do not fold in half. Wrap one section around two looped pieces to form bows and secure with edible glue. Set aside on foam to dry.

6 Using the kit box heart-shaped templates, scribe a heart on the top of each cake, using the correct size for each.

Lace

7 Mark diagonal lines across each square on the squared paper. Cover with a piece of butcher's wrap or non-stick paper and attach both to a firm board. Using royal icing and the No.0 tube pipe three lines, using the triangle as a guide. Repeat to make about 150 pieces. Set aside to dry.

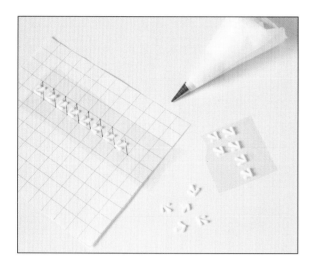

8 Using lilac royal icing and the No.1 tube, follow the scribed heart shape on the top of the cake and pipe tiny dots, leaving a gap after every fourth dot. In this gap pipe three tiny dots with white royal icing and the No.0 tube to form a triangle.

9 Pipe lilac dots in a similar way on the scribed curves on the sides of the cakes but instead of piping three white dots in the gaps, attach a piece of lace at a 45° angle, securing it with a dot of royal icing.

Assembling the cakes

10 Secure a ball of white modelling paste to the centre back of each cake. Wire the iris, buds, white blossoms and foliage together to make six small sprays. Attach one spray to each side of the ball of paste. Attach a bow with edible glue, pressing gently so that it sits neatly on top of the ball of paste and in between the flowers. *Take great care not to damage the flowers when attaching the bows.*

11 Trim the cake boards with the lilac ribbon and lightly dust the edge of the boards with lilac dusting power to accentuate the 'silk' texture. Arrange the cakes offset on perspex stands, as they do not stack.

Wiring Sprays

Putting together your flowers once you have made them is a skill on its own — I could write another book on that area of sugarcraft alone! However, here are a few hints to help you achieve good results.

Flower arranging books are very helpful, as is lots of practice. I recommend using silk flowers to practise wiring, as these will not be as delicate as your sugar ones. You can take them apart and rewire as many times as you like until you have just the right shape.

Posy

A posy is a very traditional, easy way of arranging flowers. Use a small ball of paste or circle of styrene as a base and insert wired ribbons and flowers around the lower outer edge. Make one side of the arrangement a mirror image of the other if you wish.

Gradually add more flowers and ribbons to fill out the centre of the posy. The outer edge of the arrangement should form a definite curve — imagine it has to fit inside a half ball shape.
(Posy from Special Memories on page 84)

Sprays

Sprays, or returns as they are sometimes called, give length and width to arrangements and can be attached to wired or fixed posies to change and extend the shape.

Start with a single long wire with a small bud or leaf on one end. Tape small leaves, buds, flowers and ribbons along the length of the wire on either side, increasing the size of the flowers and leaves as you get to the other end of the wire. In other words, you are recreating how a stem of real flowers and leaves would look, with the new growth, i.e. the smallest leaves and buds, at the tip.

When two sprays are added to a small wired posy the shape of the arrangement is totally changed.

Once the sprays are added they can be positioned to form different shaped arrangements: a crescent can be made by curving two sprays in the centre; an S shape is simply achieved by curving one spray to form the top of the S and a second spray the opposite way to complete it.

When two sprays are arranged as they are in the picture below, it is known as a straight bouquet.

NOTE
When decorating cakes with wired flower sprays it is important to use flower picks. A hollow flower pick should be pressed into the cake and the wired spray inserted into the pick. This is to ensure that the wires do not make direct contact with the cake. It is also vital to inform the recipient of the cake that a pick has been used. I usually attach a note to the cake box.

Love's Dream

*Pink is a popular choice for many brides. The soft pleating
and subtle brush embroidery make this a very pretty cake.*

CAKE AND DECORATION MATERIALS
*25 x 20cm (10 x 8 in), 20 x 15cm (8 x 6 in) and
15 x 10cm (6 x 4 in) oval cakes
apricot glaze
2.75kg (5½lb) almond paste
clear alcohol (gin or vodka) for brushing
2kg (4lb) pale pink sugarpaste
125g (4oz) soft peak royal icing
piping gel (see page 10)
250g (8oz) pale pink modelling paste
edible glue (see page 11)*

EQUIPMENT
*33 x 28cm (13 x 11in), 28 x 23cm (11 x 9in)
and 25 x 18cm (9 x 7 in) oval cake boards
side stencil (see Note)
No.1 or No.0 plain piping tube (tip)
foam pad for pleating
thin wooden skewers*

FINISHING TOUCHES
*3 lilies and 3 buds (see page 45)
white filler flowers
6 lily leaves
3 sprays of variegated ivy
claret florist wire
3m x 1cm (3yd x ½ in) wide white ribbon*

∽ Preparing the cakes ∾

1 Brush the cakes with apricot glaze and
cover with almond paste. Leave to dry.
Brush the almond paste with alcohol, then
cover the cakes and boards with sugarpaste.
Leave to dry for three days. Attach the cakes
to the boards with a little royal icing.

2 Measure the circumference of each cake
to determine how much of the stencil
design will fit into each quarter. Hold the
stencil carefully against the side of the cake
with the bottom edge resting on the board.
Transfer the design to the side of the cake by

~ 76 ~

scribing around the inside edge of the pattern. Adjust the position of the stencil to centre the design within each quarter section of the cake.

⊂ō *Brush embroidery* ⊂ō

3 Add the piping gel to the royal icing and fill a small parchment piping bag fitted with a No.1 or No.0 piping tube (see Note).

4 Have ready a damp cloth, a small container of water and a fine sable paintbrush. Working on one leaf or flower shape at a time, pipe around the scribed outline. Pipe a second line on top of the first. Dampen the paintbrush, flatten the tip between finger and thumb and draw the second piped line down from the top to the base. Lift off any surplus icing with the paintbrush. Repeat around all the cakes.

5 Tilt the cake and pipe the scribed underline with the No.1 tube. Add three small dots to the line work above each reverse design.

⊂ō *Pleating* ⊂ō

6 Following the detailed instructions on page 30 roll out a piece of pink modelling paste. Place an icing ruler or strip of card lightly on the paste and cut a strip the same width. Lift the strip onto a piece of foam and commence pleating. When the full length of paste has been pleated, slide it off the foam. Flatten a little way in at one side and trim.

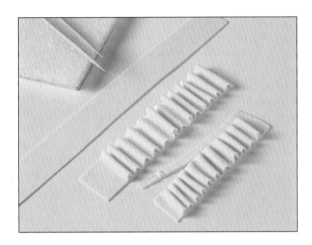

7 Moisten the cake at the base with edible glue and attach the pleated section, with the flattened edge touching the cake.

8 Repeat steps 6 and 7 to cut and pleat enough strips to trim the base of each cake.

∽ *Assembling the cakes* ∽

9 Wire together the flowers and leaves to make three sprays. Loop the florist wire at the back of each spray, and leave trailing at the front with the ivy to give added interest. Arrange a spray on one side of the top of each tier as shown. Trim the cake boards with the white ribbon. Arrange the cakes offset on a perspex stand.

NOTE
Several different designs are now available for stencilling — simply choose one that you like.

It is entirely up to you whether you use a No.0 or No.1 piping tube for the brush embroidery, depending on your skill and confidence in piping and how often you use a No.0 tube.

Laura

The perfect wedding present. The all-over stencilling and large bows make this a gift of a cake for those decorators who feel that flower making is not for them. Cold porcelain flowers, though inedible, can be used for table decorations, corsages, etc. to great effect. Here I have used a spray of yellow porcelain roses intertwined with coiled thin silver ribbon as a simple decoration for the cake board. Alternatively, a silk spray could be used.

CAKE AND DECORATION MATERIALS
30cm (12 in) and 20cm (8 in) square cakes
apricot glaze
3.5kg (7lb) almond paste
clear alcohol (gin or vodka) for brushing
3kg (6lb) cream sugarpaste
60g (2oz) soft peak royal icing
cream dusting powder (petal dust)
375g (12oz) cream modelling paste
edible glue (see page 11)

EQUIPMENT
38cm (15 in) square thin gold cake board and
23cm (9 in) square thin silver cake board
large flower stencil
No. 2 plain piping tube (tip)
1m x 1cm (1yd x ½ in) wide stiff gold net ribbon
rose wire

FINISHING TOUCHES
spray of porcelain or silk yellow roses
thin silver ribbon (optional)

❧ Stencilling ❧

It is essential to practise stencilling before attempting it on a cake. Use paper or a covered board to practise on. This will enable you to gauge the depth of colour you want to achieve and the stencilling technique that you prefer. Stencilling can be worked by using an airbrush, powder colours, or mixed paste colourings and white vegetable fat (shortening) or petal cream.

❧ Preparing the cakes ❧

1 Brush the cakes with apricot glaze and cover with almond paste. Leave to dry. Brush the almond paste with alcohol, then cover the cakes with cream sugarpaste. Leave to dry for three days. Attach to the boards with a little royal icing. Place the smaller cake on top of the larger cake in the back corner (see main picture) and secure with royal icing.

2 Hold the stencil firmly on the cake and, using cream dusting powder lightened with cornflour if necessary, brush the colour onto the large cake through the stencil.

3 Using the No.2 piping tube and white or cream soft peak royal icing, pipe a snail's trail around the base of both cakes.

⌦ *Ribbons* ⌫

4 Roll out the modelling paste quite thinly and cut a strip 3.5cm (1½ in) wide and long enough to fit up and over the large

cake. Offset the ribbon and attach with edible glue. Cut another ribbon and attach to the other side of the cake (see main picture).

5 Repeat step 4 to cut ribbons for the top tier, but stencil and colour before attaching to the cake.

⌦ *Ribbon loops* ⌫

6 You will require a minimum of twenty-five loops to achieve the size of bows shown. The number and variety will depend on whether you want a largely plain bow or a highly patterned one. Cut strips 2.5cm (1 in) wide and 7.5 to 10cm (3 to 4 in) long. Brush one end of the strips with edible glue and wrap around small pieces of foam to form loops. Repeat the procedure but stencil the strips before folding.

⌦ *Assembling the bows* ⌫

7 Arrange a minimum of five loops in a circle (the foam can be left in) overlapping the flattened edges to join. Using royal icing or edible glue, attach further loops to the inside and so on until a nice big bow is formed. Mix and match the stencilled and plain loops as you desire. When the loops are firm, remove the foam supports.

8 Cut pieces of gold net ribbon and form loops slightly smaller than those made of paste. Use rose wire to twist the ends together. Position these loops in the finished bow.

9 Arrange the spray of roses, intertwined with coiled silver ribbon if desired, along one side of the cake board.

TIP
Use an icing ruler to ensure you achieve a straight edge when cutting out the ribbons.

Special Memories

The use of gold and white gives an opulent feel to this beautiful two tier wedding cake. Tulle fans, pearls and white silk leaves add a light and airy touch to the posies, and delicate oriental stringwork completes the picture.

CAKE AND DECORATION MATERIALS

25cm (10 in) and 15cm (6 in) round cakes
apricot glaze
2kg (4lb) almond paste
clear alcohol (gin or vodka) for brushing
1.5kg (3lb) white sugarpaste
125g (4oz) soft peak royal icing
1.5m x 2.5cm (1½yd x 1 in) wide white pearlised ribbon with gold edging and 1.5m x 5mm (1½yd x ¼ in) wide gold ribbon to trim cakes
60g (2oz) modelling paste
edible glue (see page 11)
gum arabic and liquid glucose

EQUIPMENT

33cm (13 in) and 23cm (9 in) round cake boards
ivy leaf embosser
No.0 plain piping tube (tip)

FINISHING TOUCHES

6 cream full blown large sugar roses and 6 buds
15 large cream silk leaves
10 sprays of cream Gypsophilia
10 cream organza wired ribbon loops (see page 57)
1.5m x 1cm (1½yd x ½ in) wide white ribbon

⬳ *Preparing the cakes* ⬳

1 Brush the cakes with apricot glaze and cover with almond paste. Leave to dry. Brush the almond paste with alcohol, then cover the cakes and boards with sugarpaste. Leave to dry for three days. Attach the cakes to the boards with a little royal icing.

2 Attach the white gold-edged ribbon around the base of the cakes with a little royal icing.

⬳ *Embossing* ⬳

3 Roll out a strip of modelling paste at least 2.5cm (1 in) wide and indent along the centre of the strip with the ivy leaf embosser. (If the indentations are not very prominent it will probably be because the paste has been rolled too thinly.) Using an icing ruler and a sharp kitchen knife, cut out the strip as neatly as possible. Cut the end at an angle so that when the next piece is attached the join will not be noticeable. Attach to the cake above the ribbon using edible glue. Repeat until both cakes are

encircled with strips. Attach the narrow gold ribbon above the embossed strips with royal icing.

4 Using soft peak royal icing and the No.0 tube, pipe small dots around the cakes at 1cm (½ in) intervals along the bottom edge of the embossed strip. These will form the base supports for the oriental stringwork.

⌘ *Piped embroidery* ⌘

5 Pipe an ivy leaf design freehand around the cakes. Use the piped dots as a marker to maintain size.

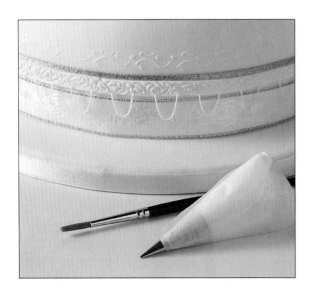

⌘ *Oriental stringwork* ⌘

Have ready a fine sable paintbrush, a small container of water and a damp cloth. Add a pinch of gum arabic and ¼ tsp liquid glucose to the royal icing to improve its elasticity.

6 Using the No.0 tube and ensuring that the tip is always clean, drop a loop from one of the piped dots to the next. The bottom edge of the loop should be approximately 2.5cm (1 in) above the cake board. Pipe the next loop so the bottom edge is about 1.5cm (¾ in) above the board. Continue to form this first set of loops around both cakes, alternating the depth as indicated.

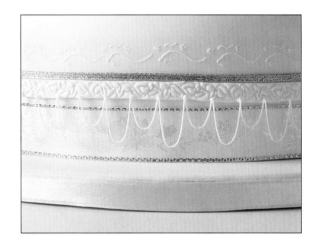

7 Pipe a second row of loops on top of the longer loops only, this time dropping the loop slightly lower than the first. Leave to dry.

8 Very carefully turn the cakes upside down and rest them on a piece of thin foam on a stand or turntable. Pipe a row of loops corresponding to the shorter piped loops, extending them down to the gold ribbon and forming an oval shape (see top left picture on facing page).

9 Turn the cakes right way up and work the embroidered ivy design (see step 5) around the top edge of the bottom tier only (see main picture).

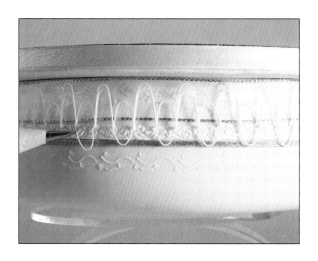
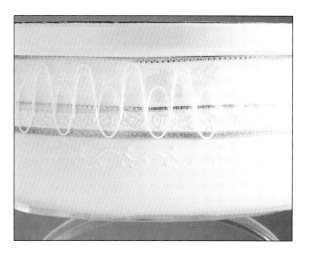

⸮ *Assembling the cakes* ⸮

10 Make two posies of roses, buds, leaves, Gypsophilia and wired ribbon loops and attach to the cakes as shown (see also page 74). Trim the cake boards with the white ribbon. Arrange the top tier offset on a perspex stand.

Lilac Delight

The unusual trellis pieces on the sides of the cakes take time and patience but the end result is well worth the effort.

CAKE AND DECORATION MATERIALS

*25cm (10 in), 20cm (8 in) and 15cm (6 in) long
octagonal cakes
apricot glaze
3kg (6lb) almond paste
3kg (6lb) white sugarpaste
500g (1lb) lilac sugarpaste
60g (2oz) soft peak royal icing
500g (1lb) modelling paste, coloured lilac with
grape violet paste colouring
lilac and plum dusting powders (petal dusts)
edible glue (see page 11)
125g (4oz) flower paste
leaf green and chestnut brown paste colourings*

EQUIPMENT

*33cm (13 in) long octagonal cake board
two 28cm (11 in) long thin octagonal cake boards
trellis design side stencil
No. 2 plain piping tube (tip)
blossom cutters
tea-strainer or small piece of tulle
maidenhair fern cutter*

FINISHING TOUCHES

*9 wired Scabious and 5 buds
2 sprays of small and medium needlepoint ivy
leaves and 5 large leaves
9 white buds and 7 filler flowers
wired ribbon loops (see page 57)
0.5m x 1cm (½ yd x ½ in) wide white ribbon*

⚭ Preparing the cakes ⚭

1 Brush the cakes with apricot glaze and cover with almond paste. Leave to dry. Brush the almond paste with alcohol, then cover the cakes with white sugarpaste. Leave to dry for three days. Cover all the cake boards with lilac sugarpaste and set aside to dry. Attach the cakes to the boards with a little royal icing.

⚭ Trellis work ⚭

2 Roll out a strip of lilac modelling paste and lay it on top of the trellis stencil. Press the paste along the length of the stencil so that it is forced gently into the cut-out sections. When you have pressed along the

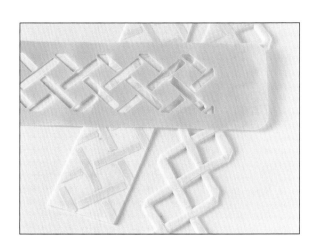

complete strip turn the paste over, making sure the stencil stays attached. If you want the trellis a little darker brush on some lilac dusting powder.

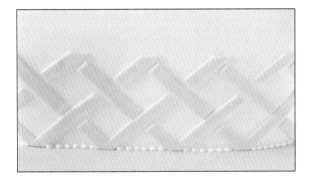

✑ *Cutting out* ✑

3 Commence cutting from the outside in but do not cut the tiny gaps at the ends of the trellis for the moment. When all the square segments and outer pieces have been removed, brush the back sparingly with edible glue. Very carefully attach the trellis to the sides of the cake, making sure that the lines are straight. Cut out the remainder of

the background paste once the trellis is in position on the cake.

4 Repeat steps 2 and 3 to cut and attach trellis to all three cakes, taking particular cake to trim correctly when joining sections. Allow plenty of time to cut out the background paste or the end result will look messy.

5 Pipe a snail's trail of royal icing at the base of the cakes in between the trellis work if desired.

✑ *Scabious* ✑

If possible, use a picture of a scabious as a colour guide.

6 Colour half of the flower paste lilac with grape violet paste colouring and half leaf green with leaf green paste colouring. Using the lilac flower paste, roll out and cut two large blossoms. Frill around the edges with a celpin or cocktail stick. Stick one of top of the other with edible glue.

7 Add a tiny piece of green flower paste to some lilac paste and knead together. Roll out and cut a small blossom. Frill and attach to the top of the two larger blossoms.

8 For the centre, push some of the same colour paste through a tea-strainer or a piece of tulle and attach. Leave to dry then dust with a mixture of lilac and plum dusting powders. Repeat to make seven unwired scabious for the cake sides (see main picture). A wired version of the same flower is used in the sprays.

ᴄᴏ *Maidenhair fern* ᴄᴏ

9 Add a touch of chestnut brown paste colouring to some green flower paste to soften the colour (again a photograph of the real thing is useful). Roll out very thinly and cut out some of the leaves. Ball around the edges to soften and set aside to dry. Approximately fifty leaves in varying sizes are required.

10 When the flowers and leaves are dry, attach them to the sides of the cakes and the boards with a little royal icing, arranging them as shown.

ᴄᴏ *Assembling the cakes* ᴄᴏ

11 Wire together the flowers, foliage and wired ribbon loops to make two sprays. Attach to the top and bottom tiers as shown. Trim the largest cake board with the white ribbon. The trellis work on these cakes is shown to best advantage when the cakes are slightly offset and fairly close together. Because of the larger boards they would not look balanced if stacked.

NOTE
Practise making the trellis work a few times before attempting this cake as it is important to achieve a satisfactory thickness: too thick and the end result will look heavy when attached to the cake, too thin and the paste will not go through the stencil. To get a clean edge when cutting out, use a scalpel if you can, or put a new blade in your craft knife.

Almond Favours

Almond favours have become a popular feature of English weddings. Originally a European tradition, the favours are small bundles of tulle enclosing five sugar-coated almonds, signifying health, wealth, happiness, love and fertility. They are given to female guests, usually by the bride, as a token of the wedding and make a delightful gift.

If you wish to present them to male guests, use small boxes shaped like top hats. For children, use novelty boxes.

The traditional favours are really easy to make. Simply gather together two or three tulle circles and tie with ribbons. Add small flowers or trinkets if you wish. Place the almonds in a small plastic container to hold them firm in the tulle.

A wide selection of tulle circles in pastel colours as well as patterned lace can be obtained from good stockists. Use one patterned circle and one or two plain ones, matching the colours of the tulle and ribbons with the bridesmaids' dresses and overall theme.

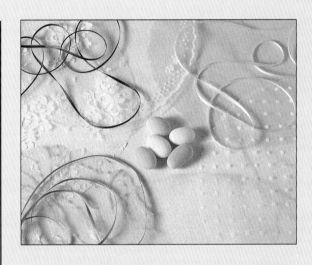

Make sure that the circles are tied tightly so that the tulle can be pulled to fan out at the top. It is possible to hire a machine that will bind the circles for you, which is very useful if you have hundreds of guests.

Almond Favour Box

A handmade almond favour makes a lovely gift. This delightful pleated box would be suitable to make for a small number of guests or if you have plenty of time. It has been created to match the Springtime cake on page 26, but can be trimmed with any flowers you wish, see below. You will need approximately 60g (2oz) modelling paste.

1 Roll out a medium size ball of paste to about 5mm (¼ in) thick. Cut an oval approximately 6cm (2½ in) and set aside to dry.

2 Roll out another piece of modelling paste quite thinly and cut a strip 3.5cm (1½ in) wide and about 15cm (6 in) long. Following the detailed instructions on page 30, pleat the strip.

3 Glue around the edge of the oval and stand the pleated section up against it, pressing to secure.

4 Repeat steps 2 and 3 to pleat and attach another strip.

5 To make the lid, cut a piece of paste 5cm (2 in) wide and 15cm (6 in) long. Pleat as before. While the pleats are still soft, pinch the ends of the strip in towards the middle and glue so that they fan out at the end. The finished lid should be slightly larger than the base. Decorate the top of the lid with small balls of paste and flowers, as desired.

In the Pink

Soft pinks are the order of the big day with this dainty two tier cake. The broderie anglaise design adds colour and texture.

CAKE AND DECORATION MATERIALS
*20cm (8 in) and 15cm (6 in) round cakes
apricot glaze
1.75kg (3½lb) almond paste
clear alcohol (gin or vodka) for brushing
1.25kg (2½lb) white sugarpaste
500g (1lb) pink sugarpaste
60g (2oz) soft peak royal icing
250g (8oz) pink modelling paste
edible glue (see page 11)
claret food colouring*

EQUIPMENT
*28cm (11 in) and 23cm (9 in) round cake boards
plaque cutter
plunger blossom cutters
small leaf cutter
Nos.0, 1, 2 and 3 plain piping tubes (tips)
celpin*

FINISHING TOUCHES
*10 large pale pink silk roses
about 12 medium sugar leaves
Gypsophilia
8 pink net ribbon loops (see page 37)
1.5m x 1cm (1½yd x ½ in) wide white ribbon*

∽ *Preparing the cakes* ∽

1 Brush the cakes with apricot glaze and cover with almond paste. Leave to dry. Brush the almond paste with alcohol, then cover the cakes with white sugarpaste. Leave to dry for three days. Cover the cake boards with pink sugarpaste and set aside to dry. Attach the cakes to the boards with a little royal icing.

∽ *Broderie anglaise* ∽

2 Roll out a golf ball size piece of pink modelling paste and, using the plaque cutter, cut out one shaped piece. Cut in half lengthways with a sharp knife.

3 Following the main picture for guidance, cut out a centre flower from the plaque using the largest of the plunger blossom cutters, then cut out two small leaves on either side. Cut out tiny holes around the top edge using the No.3 piping tube or a drinking straw. Prick the paste in between these holes with the celpin.

4 Measure the circumference of one cake, divide into four and mark the quarters on the side and top of the cake, so that the top quarters fall between the bottom quarters.

5 Brush the back of the plaque sparingly with edible glue and attach to the top of the cake on a marked point.

6 Repeat steps 2, 3, 4 and 5 to cut and attach fifteen more plaques to the top and side of both cakes. Attach the side pieces with the flat edge resting along the base of the cake, touching the board.

7 Using a No.0 or No.1 tube and white royal icing, pipe a flower, dot and scroll design around the edge of the plaques.

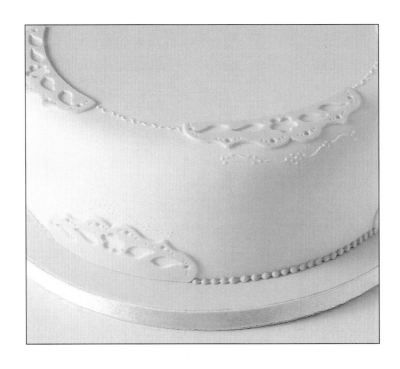

8 Colour some royal icing pink with a touch of claret food colouring. Using the No.2 tube, pipe a snail's trail around the base of the cakes in between the plaques. Repeat the flower and dot design in pink icing between the plaques on top of the cakes if desired.

Assembling the cakes

9 Arrange the roses, leaves, ribbon loops and Gypsophilia in a lovely large posy and attach to the top tier. Trim the cake boards with the white ribbon. Position the cakes traditionally on pillars.

TIP
When colouring sugarpaste and royal icing, add the colouring a fraction at a time, particularly to royal icing, to ensure subtle results. It is easier to add a little more if the colour is too pale than to try and lighten it if it is too strong.

Fine Affair

Lace has been used to create these beautiful roses.
The translucent petals give a very delicate finish and the green
and white lace ribbon complements the tiny green leaves.

CAKE AND DECORATION MATERIALS
25 x 20cm (10 x 8 in) and 20 x 15cm (8 x 6 in)
oval cakes
apricot glaze
2kg (4lb) almond paste
1kg (2lb) soft peak royal icing
1m x 1cm (1yd x ½ in) wide lace ribbon to trim
cakes
edible glue (see page 11)
30g (1oz) white flower paste
15g (½oz) green flower paste
little white vegetable fat (shortening)
25cm (10 in) posy-frill lace, tulle or net
yellow dusting powder (petal dust)
1.5m x 1cm (1½yd x ½ in) wide white ribbon

EQUIPMENT
33 x 28cm (13 x 11 in) and 28 x 23cm (11 x 9
in) oval cake boards
1cm (½ in) squared paper
Nos.1 and 2 plain piping tubes (tips)
medium size rose leaf cutter and veiner
tiny plain leaf cutter or large drinking straw
petal templates (see page 133)
reel of white cotton
rose wire
thin strips of white stemtex (florists tape)

❧ Preparing the cakes ❧

1 Brush the cakes with apricot glaze and cover with almond paste. Attach to the cake boards and coat with royal icing. Set aside to dry. Coat the boards with royal icing.

❧ Side design ❧

2 Cut a strip of squared paper the circumference and depth of the cakes. Trace and cut the side designs on page 142 onto the templates and attach with masking tape around the side of the cakes, adapting the size to suit if necessary.

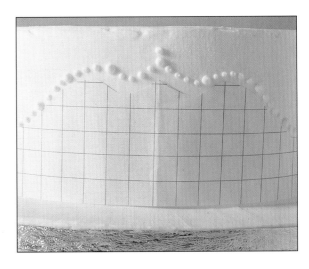

3 Using the No.1 tube (tip) and royal icing, pipe graduated dots around the cakes following the template. Pipe a snail's trail around the top edge of the cakes.

4 Attach the lace ribbon around the base of the cakes with edible glue and pipe a small bulb of icing at intervals around the base of the cakes.

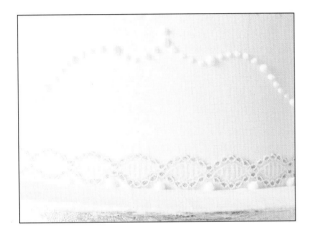

✁ *Leaves* ✁

5 Roll out a small ball of white flower paste and cut and vein fourteen rose leaves. Set aside to dry.

6 Roll out a small ball of green flower paste very thinly. Using the leaf cutter or drinking straw (with the end cut at a 45° angle) cut out twenty-four leaves. Mark a centre vein on each with the back of a craft knife.

✁ *Roses* ✁

7 Attach a piece of butcher's wrap or non-stick paper to a 15cm (6in) square piece of perspex or glass with masking tape and rub the surface with white vegetable fat. Using the petal templates, cut out fourteen large and three small petals from the lace, tulle or net. Smooth them onto the prepared paper.

8 Using the No.2 tube and soft peak royal icing, pipe an outline around the edge of each petal, then pipe some veins on the lace with the No.1 tube. Set aside to dry thoroughly.

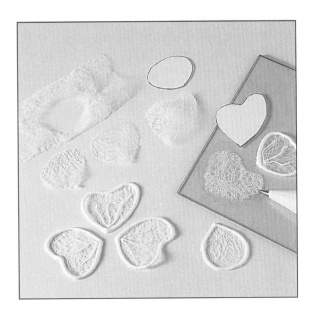

✁ *Rose stamen* ✁

9 Wrap some white cotton around your index and middle finger about twenty-five times to form loops. Twist into a figure of eight and hook a small piece of rose wire over each end. Tape with white stemtex to hold the cotton. Cut the loops to form bundles of stamen. Lightly brush the ends of the cotton with edible glue and dip into

yellow dusting powder. Make four bundles of stamen, one for each flower.

10 Carefully remove the lace petals from the paper. Using the No.1 tube, pipe a small bulb of royal icing on the underside point of each petal. Arrange three groups of three large petals on the large cake and support the outside edges with small pieces

of foam until dry. Attach white rose leaves on either side of the petals and two groups of three small green leaves on either side of those (see main picture).

11 Arrange and attach five large petals to the centre of the small cake as shown below, supporting the outside edges with foam. Leave to dry.

12 Attach three small petals to the centre of the first set, securing with royal icing. Arrange and attach three white rose leaves on either side of the rose and two groups of three green leaves either side of those.

13 Pipe a bulb of white royal icing in the centre of each flower and attach the stamen.

∽ *Assembling the cakes* ∾

14 Trim the cake boards with the white ribbon. Arrange the cakes offset on a perspex stand.

TIP
When large decorations such as these roses are used, it is preferable to offset the cakes for display. This enables the flowers to be seen clearly to their best advantage and not be overshadowed by another tier.

IMPORTANT NOTE
As the bundles of stamen and petals are inedible, please ensure they are removed from the cakes before serving.

True Love

Tiny red roses and leaves highlight the clean lines and cornelli work on this delicate two-tier wedding cake. The heart-shaped cake top ornament is made from pastillage and decorated to complement the cake.

CAKE AND DECORATION MATERIALS
25cm (10 in) and 20cm (8 in) round cakes
apricot glaze
2.5kg (5lb) almond paste
1kg (2lb) soft peak royal icing
30g (1oz) each light green, dark green and white flower paste
edible glue (see page 11)
125g (4oz) red flower paste
2m x 1cm (2yd x ½ in) wide white ribbon

EQUIPMENT
33cm (13 in) and 28cm (11 in) round cake boards
Kit Box scalloped templates
Nos.0 and 1 plain piping tubes (tips)
quilling cutter
26-gauge wires
2.5cm (1in) blossom cutter
tiny rose leaf cutter
Dresden tool
heart-shaped template (see page 141)
medium size plain leaf cutter
1.5cm (¾ in) round cutter

∽ Preparing the cakes ∾

1 Brush the cakes with apricot glaze and cover with almond paste. Attach to the cake boards and coat with royal icing. Set aside to dry. Coat the boards with royal icing.

∽ Cornelli work ∾

2 Measure the circumference of each cake and divide into five sections, marking the edge of the cake top. Using the approximate size Kit Box template, scribe five scallops around the side of each cake.

3 Using the No.0 tube and slightly softened royal icing, pipe cornelli work beneath the scallops and all over the boards

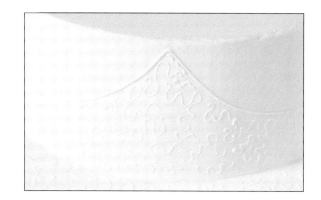

as shown. Tilt the cakes and pipe a line over the scribed scallops around the side of the cakes.

∽ *Ribbons* ∽

4 Roll out a small ball of light green flower paste quite thinly and cut ribbon strips with the quilling cutter. They should be slightly shorter than the depth of the cakes with the ends cut at an angle. Attach two strips to the top of each scallop on both cakes with edible glue.

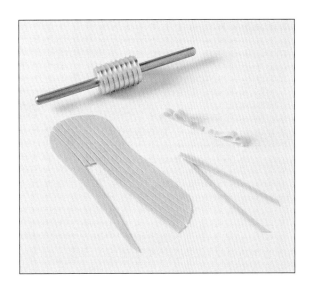

5 To make the loops, cut another strip of paste 7.5cm (3 in) long. Fold one end over to form a small loop and secure with edible glue. Lift the centre of the strip and secure to form a second loop which is slightly shorter and sits on top of the first loop. Attach to the top edge of the cake just to one side of the tails. Cut and fold another strip the same length and attach to the other side of the tails as shown above right.

6 Repeat step 5 to make and attach further sets of loops to the top of the ribbon tails on both cakes.

7 Using the No.1 tube and royal icing, pipe a snail's trail around the top edge of the cakes between the bows.

∽ *Roses and leaves* ∽

8 Cut some pieces of wire 7.5cm (3 in) long. (These are used for ease of assembly but are removed after completion of the flower.) Form a tiny cone of red flower paste on the end of a wire. Repeat to make ten more. Leave to dry for a few hours.

9 Roll out a small ball of red flower paste very thinly and cut two blossoms. Take one of the blossoms, ball around the edges to soften and thread a cone through the middle. Lightly brush some glue on the blossom and wrap the individual petals to form a tiny rose: wrap one petal completely around the cone, two alternate petals into the centre around the first, then the remaining two to overlap the previous two. Ball the second blossom and attach to the underside of the flower, curving the petals back slightly.

10 Repeat step 9 to make eleven complete roses. When the outer petals are dry, gently slide each rose off the wire and set aside to dry completely.

11 Roll out a small ball of dark green flower paste and cut twenty-two tiny rose leaves. Mark a centre vein with the Dresden tool or the back of a craft knife.

12 Attach a rose to the centre of the ribbon loops and a leaf on either side with royal icing.

∽ *Cake top ornament* ∾

13 Roll out a medium size ball of white flower paste to 2.5mm (⅛ in) thick. Cut a narrow strip and lay it around the outline of the heart template. Overlap the ends slightly and join with edible glue. Make a small hole at the point of the heart and insert a small piece of uncooked dried spaghetti. Set aside to dry for at least twenty-four hours. Drying the heart shape on foam or sponge will ensure both sides dry evenly.

14 Roll out a small ball of white flower paste to the same thickness and cut four medium size leaves and a small circle. Glue the leaves around the circle to form a base. Make a hole in the centre.

15 Attach ribbons, loops, a rose and leaves to the top of the heart with royal icing.

16 Pipe a small quantity of royal icing into the hole in the base and carefully position the heart by inserting the spaghetti. Support in an upright position with foam for 24 to 36 hours until completely dry.

✺ *Assembling the cakes* ✺

17 Trim the cake boards with the white ribbon. Secure the cake top ornament to the top tier with royal icing or leave free-standing. Arrange the cakes offset on a perspex stand as shown or one on top of the other on pillars.

TIP
A picture of a rose would be useful when wrapping the blossom petals to form the flower.

Grace

Ideal for the small informal wedding or for those tying the knot for the second time around. The oriental stringwork shows up well against the coloured band, while the interesting lace design, pastillage shells and lily sprays make for a colourful theme.

CAKE AND DECORATION MATERIALS

250g (8oz) sugarpaste coloured with spruce green paste colouring
25cm (10 in) long hexagonal cake
apricot glaze
1.5kg (3lb) almond paste
clear alcohol (gin or vodka) for brushing
1kg (2lb) cream-coloured sugarpaste
125g (4oz) soft peak royal icing
½ tsp gum tragacanth
edible glue (see page 11)
gum arabic and liquid glucose

EQUIPMENT

33cm (13 in) long hexagonal cake board
leaf design embosser
lace cutter
Nos.0 and 1 plain piping tubes (tips)

FINISHING TOUCHES

3 lilies (see page 45)
5 lily leaves
3 cornflowers
10 white filler flowers
3 sprays of foliage
wired ribbon loops (see page 57)
1m x 1cm (1yd x ½ in) wide picot-edged white ribbon

❧ Preparing the cake ❧

1 Cover the cake board with green sugarpaste and emboss around the edge. Ensure that even pressure is applied each time the embosser is pressed onto the paste to achieve a smooth, neat finish. Set aside to dry.

2 Brush the cake with apricot glaze and cover with almond paste. Leave to dry. Brush the almond paste with alcohol, then cover with cream sugarpaste. Leave to dry for three days. Attach the cake to the board

with a little royal icing, positioning it off centre to allow a spray of flowers to sit on the board at the front of the cake (see main picture).

3 Knead the gum tragacanth into the remaining green sugarpaste — this will give it more elasticity and body. Roll out a strip approximately 25cm (10 in) long and 7.5cm (3 in) wide. Place an icing ruler or straight edge on the paste. Position the lace cutter against the long edge of the ruler and press firmly to cut a section of paste. Lift carefully and attach around the base of the cake with edible glue. Repeat to cut and attach further lengths, making sure that the joins are neat. (With practice it is possible to roll out and cut a continuous length that will fit around the cake.)

∽ *Piped lace* ∽

4 Trace the lace design on page 138. Attach a piece of butcher's wrap or non-stick paper to a small piece of perspex or glass with masking tape, leaving room to slide the lace pattern underneath. Pipe the outline using the No. 1 tube. Although only three pieces are required, pipe several in case of breakages. Set aside to dry.

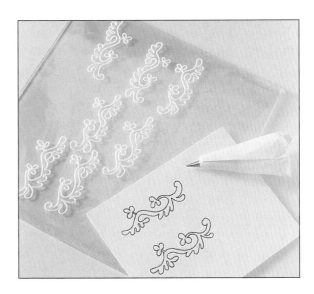

5 Colour a small quantity of soft peak royal icing with spruce green paste colouring. Fit a parchment piping bag with the No.0 tube and half fill with the icing. Pipe V shapes and tiny dots following the shape of the cut-out section on the cake.

∽ *Oriental stringwork* ∽

Please study the close-up picture of the cake side below to be sure about which loops must be piped first.

6 Have ready a fine sable paintbrush, a small container of water and a damp cloth. Add a pinch of gum arabic and ¼ tsp liquid glucose to the remaining white royal icing to improve its elasticity. Using a No.1

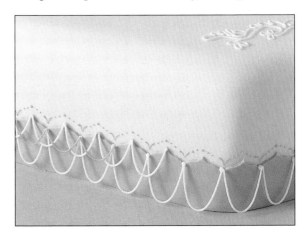

or No.0 tube (depending on which you prefer) pipe tiny dots on the green paste at the lowest and highest points of the top edge. Ensuring that the tip of the tube is always clean, drop a loop from one of the piped dots to the next on the lowest points of the design only. The bottom edge of the loops should be at least 5mm (¼ in) from the board. Continue these loops right around the cake. It is helpful to prop up the cake at the back as you work to enable the loops to stay free from the cake side.

7 Using the remaining higher dots as the point of contact, pipe a second set of shorter loops over the top of the first set.

8 Pipe a third set of loops in the green icing, making contact with the first set at the highest point.

∽ *Lace* ∾

9 Carefully remove the lace pieces from the paper with a cranked palette knife. Brush a little edible glue to the underside of the lace and attach to the top of the cake (see main picture for position).

∽ *Assembling the cake* ∾

10 Wire the flowers, foliage and wired ribbon loops together to make a small corsage and spray. Position the corsage along one side of the top of the cake and the spray on the board. To add interest, press pastillage shells out of a chocolate mould if you wish and arrange with the flowers. Trim the cake board with the white picot ribbon.

Fantasia

This impressive wedding cake was designed to reflect the style of the art deco era. The top ornament is made out of pleated sections (detailed instructions are given on page 118).

CAKE AND DECORATION MATERIALS

25 x 20cm (10 x 8 in), 20 x 15cm (8 x 6 in) and 15 x 10cm (6 x 4 in) scalloped oval cakes
apricot glaze
2.25kg (4½lb) almond paste
clear alcohol (gin or vodka) for brushing
1.75kg (3½lb) peach sugarpaste
125g (4oz) soft peak royal icing
250g (8oz) peach modelling paste
2.5m x 1cm (2½yd x ½ in) wide lace ribbon

EQUIPMENT

33 x 28cm (13 x 11 in), 28 x 23cm (11 x 9 in) and 23 x 18cm (9 x 7 in) scalloped oval cake boards
foam pad for pleating
thin wooden skewers
Kit Box scalloped templates
No.0 plain piping tube (tip)

FINISHING TOUCHES

14 peach Singapore orchids and 25 buds (see page 46)
sprays of green Gypsophilia
15 small periwinkle leaves
3m x 1cm (3yd x ½ in) wide green ribbon

⮑ Preparing the cakes ⮐

1 Brush the cakes with apricot glaze and cover with almond paste. Leave to dry. Brush the almond paste with alcohol, then cover the cakes and boards with peach sugarpaste. Leave to dry for three days. Attach the cakes to the boards with a little royal icing.

2 Cut out the templates for the side pleated sections and the top ornament in thin card (see page 142).

⮑ Side sections ⮐

3 Roll out a small ball of peach modelling paste and cut and pleat a square of paste (see page 30). Measure the depth of the cake. Trim one corner of the pleated square until it measures the same at its highest point as the depth of the cake. Pinch the pleats together.

4 Using the appropriate templates, cut and pleat as above four sections for each tier. Place on foam and leave to dry for three days.

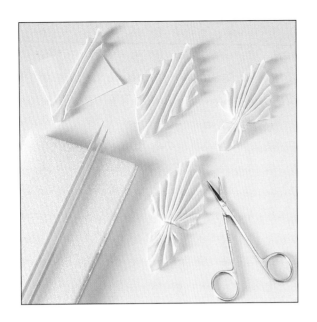

ᕙ *Cake top ornament* ᕗ

5 Pleat and cut two further sections using the smallest template and two small squares (see page 118 for detailed instructions).

ᕙ *Piped embroidery* ᕗ

6 Using a template, scribe a scallop on the sides, front and back of each cake.

7 Attach the lace ribbon to the base of the cakes with a little royal icing.

8 Tilt the cakes and pipe a line over the scribed scallop, using the No.0 tube. Using the picture as a reference, pipe a design below the line.

9 Pipe some royal icing on the back of the dried pleated sections and attach to the recesses on the sides of the cakes.

∞ *Assembling the cakes* ∞

10 Wire the flowers and foliage together to make two sprays. Attach to the underside of the bottom and middle tier cake boards and let the sprays simply rest on the cakes. Stand the cake top ornament on the top tier. Trim the cake boards with the green ribbon. Position the cakes offset on a perspex stand.

Cake Top Ornaments

The ornament that decorates the top of a wedding cake is often the first thing that people notice so it should look good and be in proportion with the cakes. Whether your decoration is large and striking or dainty and subtle will not matter as long as the overall visual effect is well balanced in both colour and shape.

A variety of options is open to you when making ornaments. You may well be asked to use a decoration that is a regular feature for family weddings. I was once asked to use an ancient chipped cherub with no hands — a real challenge! Or you may be asked to use a commercial decoration that the bride-to-be has purchased herself. Try to match flowers and ribbons wherever possible.

An easier, and to my mind a much more satisfactory, solution is to make the decoration out of modelling paste and/or flowers. The end result is much more professional. Here are a few ideas.

Pastel Magic
(page 40)

1 Roll out a large ball of white modelling paste to which a large pinch of gum tragacanth has been added. Using the template on page 141 transfer the design onto card, then carefully cut out in paste.

2 Fold in the outside edges and support with pieces of foam. Leave until completely dry. If you wish to speed up the drying time, set the whole piece aside on foam for forty-eight hours.

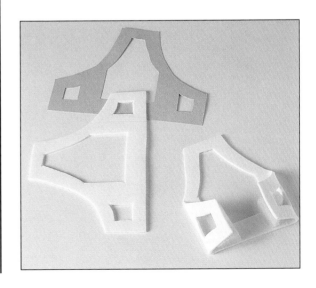

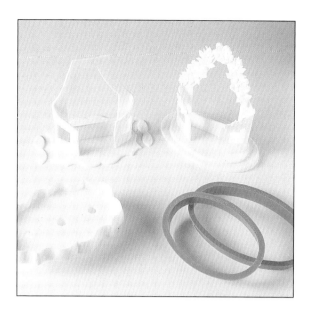

3 Using the small rose design patchwork cutter and modelling paste, cut out two complete pieces. Cut another piece but cut away the entire centre rose and the buds on each end. Attach these with edible glue while still soft to the hardened decoration.

4 Different shaped bases can also be cut out from modelling paste. Here I have used a plaque cutter with the ends removed. You can also use one or two oval cut-outs. Attach the decoration to the base with royal icing.

5 A small arrangement of silk roses together with some piped peach dots completes the decoration. The roses and rose cut-outs match those on the cakes.

Fantasia

(page 112)

1 Cut a square card template measuring at least the depth of the top tier, or more if desired.

2 Roll out a large ball of peach modelling paste and cut out two squares using the template. Pleat from corner to corner as shown on page 31. Pinch the pleats together at one corner and trim.

3 To make the base supports, cut a square template approximately half to one third of the size of the other. Cut and pleat two small squares. Curve the ends round and lift up one side. Support on foam and set aside to dry overnight.

4 Attach the base sections to the upright pieces with royal icing. Add flowers if you wish.

Pleated decoration

The decoration below is made using the pleating technique (see page 30) and two ovals as a base. The edge of the pleating and the large oval have been painted with gold food colouring. I have added scabious flowers, but any flower could be used.

NOTE
Remember — only use gold colouring
on items that can be removed from
the cake before cutting.

Regal Touch

Oriental stringwork and extension work are combined to give an elaborate side decoration. Delicate lilac sweet peas and white ivy complete the picture.

CAKE AND DECORATION MATERIALS

25cm (10 in) and 18cm (7 in) round cakes
apricot glaze
2.25kg (4½lb) almond paste
1kg (2lb) soft peak royal icing
185g (6oz) lilac modelling paste
1.5m x 1cm (1½yd x ½ in) wide lilac picot-edged ribbon to trim cakes
125g (4oz) white flower paste
edible glue (see page 11)
pale lilac dusting powder (petal dust)
2m x 1cm (2yd x ½ in) wide white ribbon

EQUIPMENT

33cm (13 in) and 25cm (10 in) round cake boards
border mould
Nos.0 and 1 plain piping tubes (tips)
sweet pea cutter
ivy leaf cutters
7.5cm (3 in) and 6cm (2½ in) oval cutters
2.5cm (1 in) round briar rose cutter

⊂ Preparing the cakes ⊃

1 Brush the cakes with apricot glaze and cover with almond paste. Attach to the cake boards and coat with royal icing. Set aside to dry. Coat the boards with royal icing.

⊂ Edging ⊃

2 Press a small ball of lilac modelling paste into a corner section of the border mould and trim. Repeat to cut about twenty-nine more pieces.

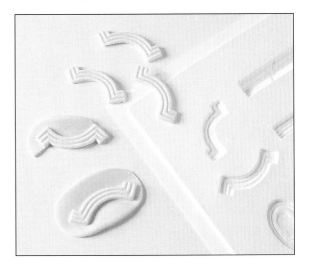

3 Measure the circumference of the cakes to determine how many of the lilac cut-outs will fit into one quarter. This will determine the size of gap you leave between them. Attach the cut-outs to the cakes with royal icing, approximately one third of the way down from the top edge, leaving a small gap between each.

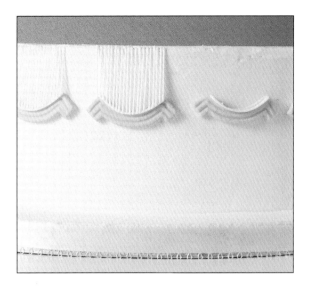

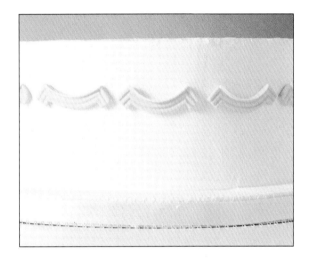

∽ *Extension work* ∾

4 Using the No.0 tube and soft peak royal icing, pipe lines down from the top edge of the cake onto the curved section of a lilac piece. Complete the extension work on one piece and then move on to the next.

Continue with care until the extension work is completed on both cakes.

∽ *Overpiping* ∾

5 Starting in the middle of the top edge of a section of the extension work, pipe a curved line that sits over the extension work and ends halfway down the last strand on the outside edge. Repeat on the other side.

6 Starting again at the same centre point, pipe another two curved lines to sit below the first two and end at the bottom edge of the outside strands.

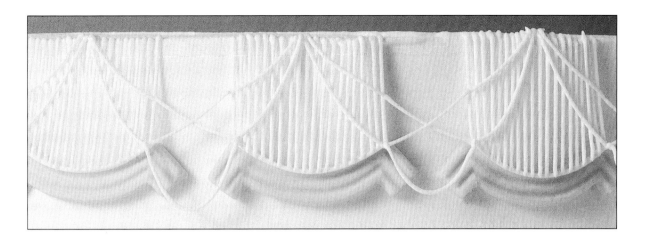

7 Repeat steps 5 and 6 to complete the overpiping on both cakes.

8 Pipe a diagonal line across the gap between the extension work from the outside edge of the upper overpiped line across to the bottom of the lower overpiped line in the next section. Reverse the procedure to pipe another diagonal line over the top of the first. This should form an X and look like a continuation of the over-piping. Now drop a piped loop under the X. Work around the cakes to complete the overpiping and oriental stringwork loops.

9 Attach the lilac ribbon carefully around the cakes about 1cm (½ in) up from the base.

⟶ *Sweet peas* ⟵

10 Roll a cone of white flower paste small enough to fit inside the smallest petal of the sweet pea cutter. Make twenty cones.

11 Roll out a small ball of white flower paste very thinly and cut out the three sections of the sweet pea. Ball the edges. Glue the smaller double petal on top of the large petal.

12 Glue the small cone to the centre of the smallest petal and fold up the sides

to enclose it completely. Glue this onto the centre of the flower to form a sweet pea. Make about twenty flowers. Leave to dry, then dust with lilac dusting powder.

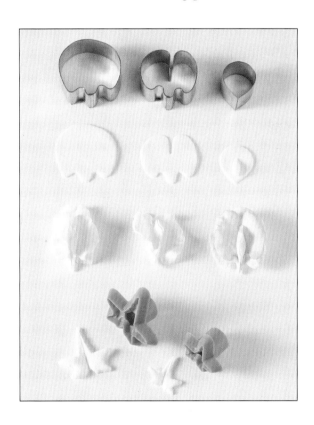

⟶ *Ivy leaves* ⟵

13 Using white flower paste, roll out and cut twenty small and twenty medium size ivy leaves. Ball to soften the edges and mark a centre vein with a Dresden tool or the back of a craft knife.

14 Taking great care not to damage the extension work, attach the sweet peas and ivy leaves alternately around the top edge of the cakes with royal icing.

☞ *Cake top ornament* ☜

15 Roll out some white flower paste to about 2.5mm (⅛ in) thick and cut a 7.5cm (3 in) oval. Using the 6cm (2½ in) cutter, cut out a centre from the large oval. Also cut out a circle of paste using the briar rose cutter.

16 Glue five cut-out lilac corner sections onto the large oval. Trim the join at one end to expose the white oval – this will slot into the base.

17 Cut the circle in half and attach to the centre of the solid oval base with royal icing, leaving a small gap between the two halves to hold the large oval. Cut out a further two lilac corner sections and, while still soft, glue them around the two half circles. Set aside to dry for at least two days.

18 Pipe a small quantity of royal icing into the gap between the two half circles and slot the oval cut-out into it. Support with foam and leave to dry. Attach leaves and sweet peas to the base and top of the ornament as shown.

∽ *Assembling the cakes* ∾

19 Attach the ornament to the top of the small cake and pipe a snail's trail around the top and base of the oval insert with the No.1 tube.

20 Trim the boards with the white ribbon. These cakes can be arranged with the smaller directly above the larger on a perspex stand, or offset.

> TIP
> *For dusting surfaces when rolling out modelling paste, use a small sterilised muslin bag filled with a 50:50 mixture of icing (confectioners') sugar and cornflour (cornstarch).*

Coffee and Cream

For those who like something different — an unusual coffee-coloured cake with a stencilled royal icing side design and all white leaves and flowers.

CAKE AND DECORATION MATERIALS

*25cm (10 in), 20cm (8 in) and 15cm (6 in)
round cakes
apricot glaze
2.75kg (5½lb) almond paste
clear alcohol (gin or vodka) for brushing
2kg (4lb) coffee-coloured sugarpaste
125g (4oz) soft peak royal icing
90g (3oz) white flower paste
edible glue (see page 11)
90g (3oz) white modelling paste
white vegetable fat (shortening)
gum tragacanth*

EQUIPMENT

*33cm (13 in), 28cm (11 in) and 23cm (9 in)
round cake boards
side stencil
small and medium rose leaf cutters
petal and rose leaf veiner
6cm (2½ in) all-in-one rose cutter
clay gun or fine tulle
No.1 plain piping tube (tip)
3m x 1cm (3yd x ½ in) wide white ribbon*

Preparing the cakes

1 Brush the cakes with apricot glaze and cover with almond paste. Leave to dry. Brush the almond paste with alcohol, then cover the cakes and boards with coffee-coloured sugarpaste. Secure the cakes very carefully to the centre of the boards whilst the sugarpaste is still soft.

2 Starting with the smallest tier, tilt the cake and hold the stencil firmly against the side at the base. Secure each end of the stencil to the cake with masking tape.

3 Ensuring that the stencil stays flat against the cake, spread soft peak royal icing along the length of the stencil in a

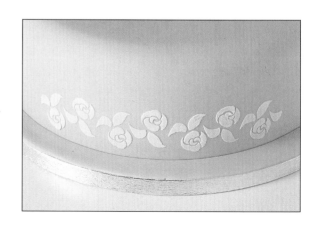

backwards and forwards action with a cranked palette knife. Remove the stencil very carefully. Repeat stencilling to complete the design around the base and on the other two cakes.

4 Roll out a small ball of white flower paste. Cut out and vein a small and medium rose leaf. Repeat to make eighteen small and four medium. Set aside to dry. Cut out and vein seven all-in-one roses; dry flat. Push some softened paste through the fine mesh of a clay gun or some tulle. Attach a small quantity to the centre of each rose.

5 For the buds, roll out and cut a rose. Cut to separate each of the petals and ball the edges to soften. Form a thin cone of paste and wrap a petal around, using glue to secure.

6 Using white modelling paste roll out eight thin sausage shapes 13cm (5 in) long, tapered at both ends. Rub a little white vegetable fat onto fingers to prevent the paste from cracking whilst rolling. Attach these in scrolls together with the roses and leaves as shown in main picture. Attach buds at random to fill gaps and finish off. Pipe dots along scrolls using the No.1 tube.

❧ *Cake top ornament* ❧

7 Rub a small amount of gum tragacanth and white vegetable fat into a golf ball size piece of modelling paste.

8 Using the template on page 141 as a shape guide, roll a sausage of paste to approximately 25cm (10 in) long and taper it at both ends. Lay the sausage shape over the top of the template, curving it into an S as shown below left. Leave to dry thoroughly.

❧ *Assembling the cakes* ❧

9 Attach the ornament upright on the cake, on one side of the top tier, securing with royal icing. Attach the two remaining roses. Trim the cake boards with the white ribbon. These cakes can be presented offset as shown but also look striking stacked one on top of the other.

NOTE
This method of attaching cake to board is good if you do not wish to pipe around the cake base. Any slight irregularities at the base of the cake are hidden when the cake is pressed into the soft sugarpaste.

It is advisable to practise this stencilling technique on a dummy or cake tin first, as removing any mistakes will mark the coloured icing.

TIP
Adding vegetable fat to modelling paste allows time to roll out the paste without it cracking. Adding gum tragacanth ensures that the finished crescent will be strong enough to stand without support.

Cloud Nine

The soft lines of cloud formations were the inspiration for this brilliant white cake. Displaying the cakes against a striking background highlights the contours of the collars.

CAKE AND DECORATION MATERIALS

*25cm (10 in), 20cm (8 in) and 15cm (6 in)
round cakes
apricot glaze
3kg (6lb) almond paste
1.25kg (2½lb) soft peak royal icing
albumen powder
60g (2oz) white modelling paste
2.5m x 1cm (2½yd x ½ in) wide white ribbon
¼ tsp gum tragacanth*

EQUIPMENT

*33cm (13 in), 28cm (11 in) and 23cm (9 in)
round cake boards
Nos.0 and 1 plain piping tubes (tips)
anglepoise lamp
tiny flower cutter (any type is suitable)
small celpin
1cm (½ in) squared paper
10cm (4 in) plaque cutter
6cm (2½ in) oval cutter*

FINISHING TOUCHES

*approx. 20 wired white lilac flowers
approx. 10 wired white lilac buds*

ᴄᴏ Preparing the cakes ᴏᴄ

1 Brush the cakes with apricot glaze and cover with almond paste. Attach to the cake boards and coat with royal icing. Set aside to dry. Coat the boards with royal icing.

ᴄᴏ Collars ᴏᴄ

2 Trace the three collar templates on page 140 onto separate pieces of white paper.

3 Place the smallest design on a piece of glass or perspex and cover with butcher's wrap or non-stick paper. Smooth out until perfectly flat and secure with masking tape. Using soft peak royal icing and the No.1 tube, pipe the outline of the design. Repeat five times to outline four for the cake top and two spares in case of breakages.

4 Thin some royal icing with albumen, adding the liquid a little at a time until you have the right consistency (see page 61). Keep the bowl covered with a damp cloth.

Half fill a medium piping bag with run-out icing. Snip off the end of the bag (to the size of a No.2 tube), hold over an empty bag and squeeze to transfer the icing from one bag to the other. This is a very good way to get rid of air bubbles (you will be able to hear them popping!).

5 Cut the same amount off this bag and commence flooding the piped design. Work on alternate sections, drying under the lamp, so that they skin over without running into each other.

6 Repeat steps 3, 4 and 5 to make six run-out collars for the middle tier and six for the bottom tier.

∽ *Flowers* ∾

7 Roll out a small ball of modelling paste quite thinly and cut out at least twenty-four tiny white flowers. Place the flowers on soft foam and press a celpin onto the centre to cup the petals. Set aside on foam to dry.

∽ *Lace* ∾

8 Using the lace pattern on page 140, soft peak royal icing and the No.0 tube, pipe approximately thirty pieces of lace onto butcher's wrap or non-stick paper. Leave to dry.

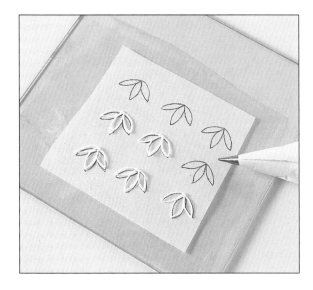

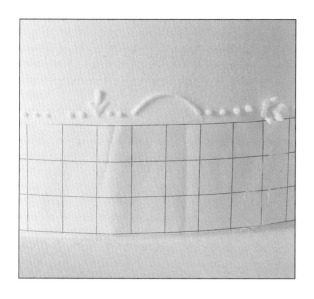

∾ *Side design* ∾

9 Cut a strip of squared paper 3cm (1¼in) wide and the circumference of the largest cake. Mark the quarters and attach around the cake as a guide for piping the side design. (See picture for side design.)

10 Using a No.0 or No.1 tube (whichever you feel most confident using), commence piping the first stage of the side design above the paper, attaching the flowers where shown.

11 Remove the squared paper and pipe the second stage of the design, which falls below the first. Attach the lace pieces as

shown. Repeat part of the design around the base of the cake as shown.

12 Repeat steps 9, 10 and 11 to complete the sides on the other two tiers, adjusting the design to fit (see Note).

13 Trim the cake boards with the white ribbon.

∾ *Attaching the collars* ∾

14 Remove the collars from the paper very carefully one at a time and attach the relevant sizes to the top of the cakes with royal icing. Position them so that they meet above the flowers at the quarter point.

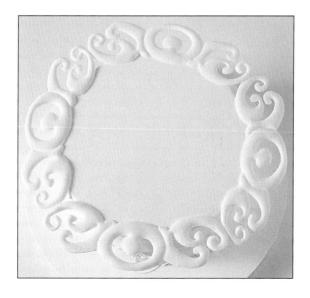

⊗ *Cake top ornament* ⊗

15 Knead the gum tragacanth into the remaining modelling paste (this will give added strength to the finished piece), then roll it out straight away to approximately 1.75mm ($^1/_{16}$ in) thick — don't roll it too thin. Cut two plaques, then cut out an oval centre from one. Set aside on foam for at least two days to dry thoroughly.

⊗ *Assembling the cakes* ⊗

16 Tape together the lilac flowers and buds and insert into a ball of modelling paste. Attach the plaques to the front and back with royal icing and secure together at one side with royal icing or a thin sausage of modelling paste to resemble an open card (make sure none of the paste can be seen). Leave to dry overnight.

17 Place the ornament in the middle of the top tier. Secure with royal icing, if desired, or leave free-standing. Arrange the cakes offset on perspex stands as shown or traditionally stacked on pillars.

NOTE
Adjust the side design to fit any size cake by reducing the number of dots piped. To ensure the designs will look balanced when the cakes are stacked, attach a flower at the quarter marks and work the design from that point.

TIP
Run-outs are best dried under an anglepoise lamp to ensure a sheen on the surface. The best way to remove run-outs from the paper is to pass a piece of very taut thread underneath them. Remove one at a time when you are ready to attach them to the cake.

Petal Shapes For Flowers

All shapes are shown actual size

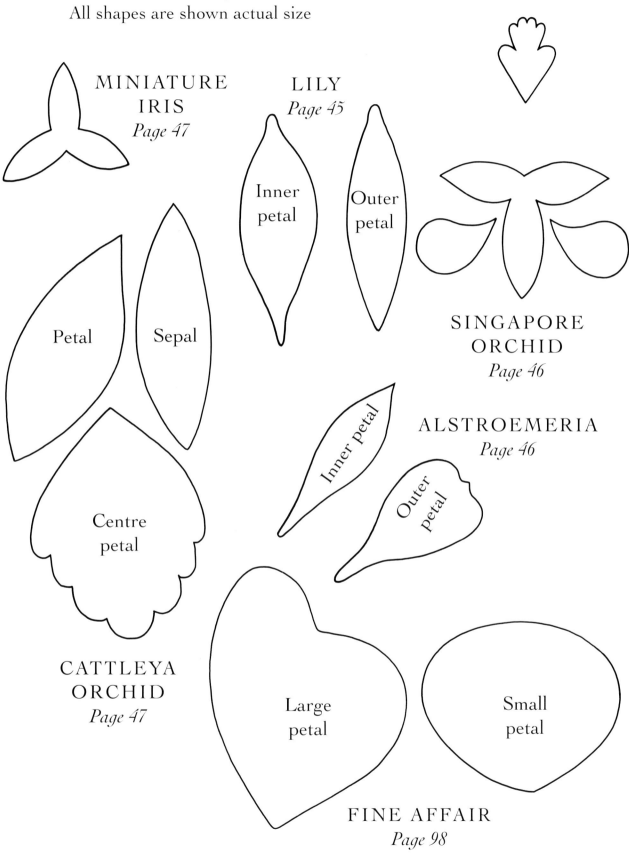

MINIATURE
IRIS
Page 47

LILY
Page 45

Inner
petal

Outer
petal

SINGAPORE
ORCHID
Page 46

Petal

Sepal

Inner petal

Outer
petal

ALSTROEMERIA
Page 46

Centre
petal

CATTLEYA
ORCHID
Page 47

Large
petal

Small
petal

FINE AFFAIR
Page 98

Cake
Presentation

The presentation of the wedding cake at the reception will depend on what the bride has in mind, what is available and what looks good.

The first thing to decide is whether the cake is to be on a separate table or set in front of the bride and groom.

If a separate table is to be used, you will need to check the size, especially if the cakes are to be offset, and the covering that is to be used. If you feel the table needs a little something extra, add your own colour co-ordinated drapes.

If the cakes are to go on the top table, arrange them so that they are not above eye level. I have frequently been to weddings where the bride and groom are peering at their guests through the top two tiers.

Two types of cake stand are now very popular: chrome and perspex. Those made from chrome are often curved and tubular. They can be decorated with silk versions of flowers incorporated on the cakes. Perspex stands give the illusion that the cakes are almost floating in mid air, which is lovely. However, perspex is expensive and scratches easily.

Traditional cake stands and pillars are still favoured by some brides and are perfect for formal royal-iced cakes. If pillars are used, it is essential to insert a skewer into the cake below each pillar to take the weight. These should not be wooden and must be removed before the cake is cut.

Some venues provide a cake stand. If they do not you will probably be able to hire one from a sugarcraft supplier.

Cutting Guide

Slicing figures for guidance only

	30cm (12 in)	25cm (10 in)	20cm (8 in)	15cm (6 in)
Round	100	80	50	35
Square	120	100	80	60
Hexagon	108	90	72	54
Petal	80	70	55	40

Templates and Patterns

When making templates for these designs use thin card where possible as it is much sturdier than greaseproof or parchment.

All templates and patterns are actual size except for Chloe which should be enlarged to 118% on a photocopier

GRACE
Page 108
Lace design

CHLOE
Page 58

Cake top edge (for royal iced cakes)

EVE
Page 48 Collar design

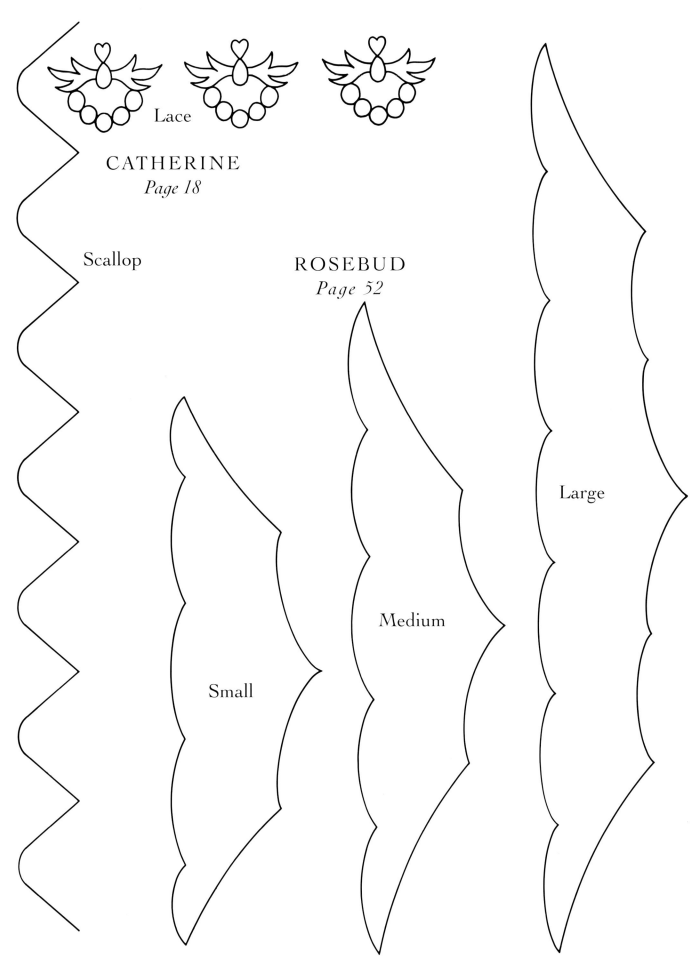

Lace

CATHERINE
Page 18

Scallop

ROSEBUD
Page 52

Large

Medium

Small

Cloud Nine templates should be
enlarged to 107% on a
photocopier

CLOUD NINE
Page 130

Large

Medium

Small

Lace design

COFFEE AND CREAM
Page 126

Cake top template

REBEKAH
Page 66
Side design

1st stage of piping

2nd stage of piping

TRUE LOVE
Page 103
Top ornament

OLD TIME
Page 32
Honeysuckle run-out

PASTEL MAGIC
Page 40 and 116

Cake top ornament

FINE AFFAIR *Page 98*
Fine Affair templates should be
enlarged to 125% on a photocopier

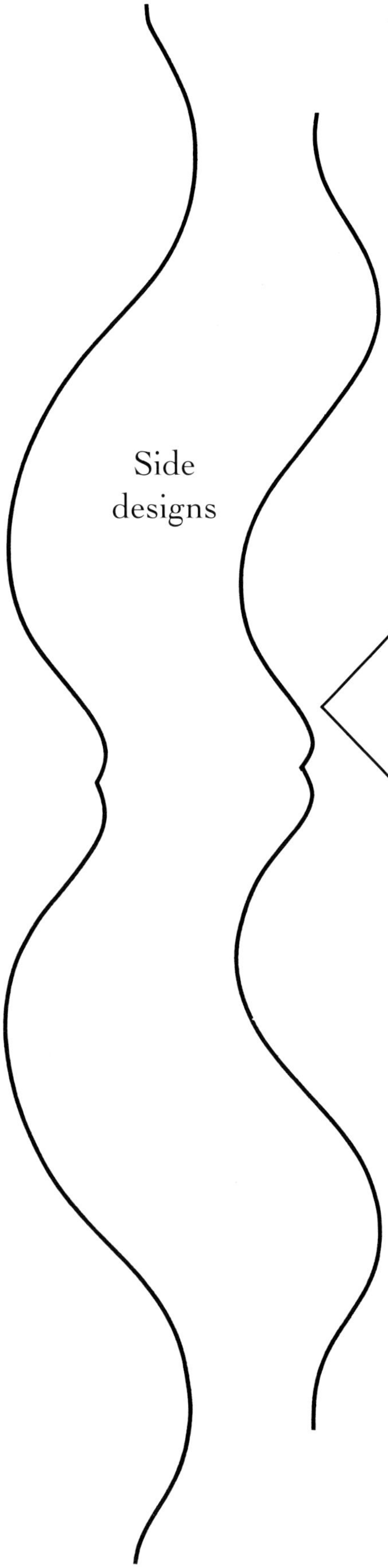

FANTASIA
Page 112

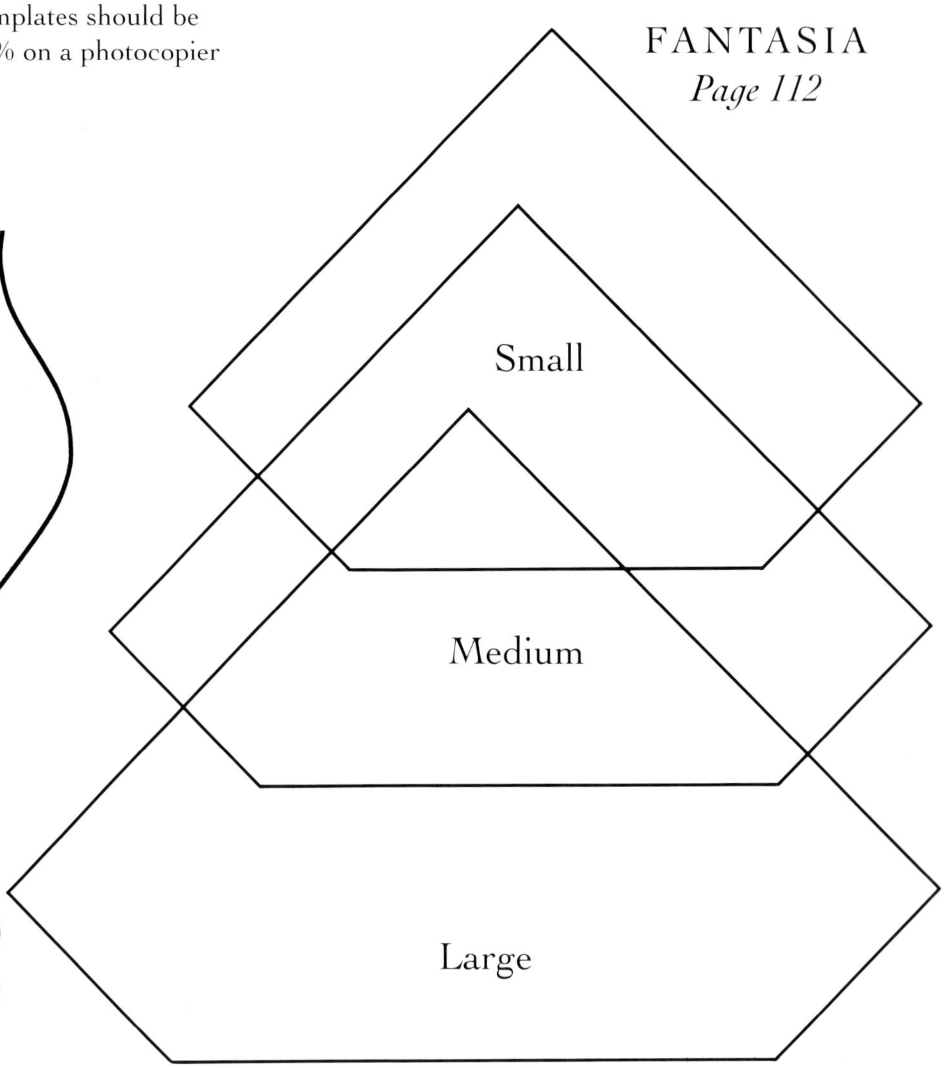

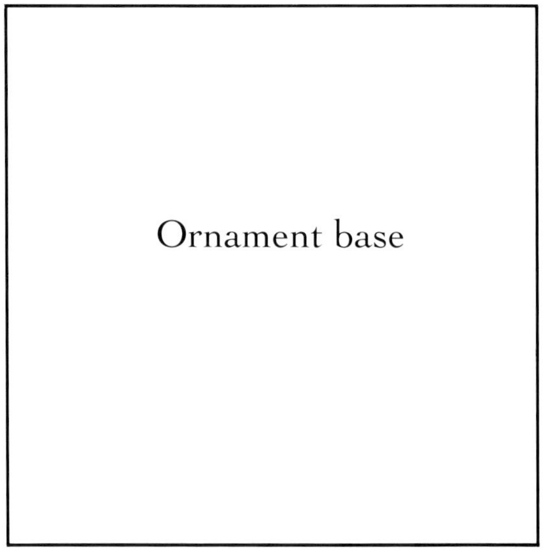

Small

Side
designs

Medium

Large

Ornament base

Index

Acknowledgements

The author and publishers would like to thank the following for their help in the production
of this book, particularly Debbie Welsh:

Creative Stencil Designs
Flanders Moss
Station Road
Buchlyvie
Stirlingshire
Tel 01360-850389

DIY Icing Centre
8 Edwards Road
Erdington
Birmingham B24 9EP
Tel & Fax 0121-384-8236

Celcakes
Springfield House
Gate Helmsley
York
North Yorkshire YO4 1NF
Tel 01759-371447
Fax 01759-372513

E.T.Webb
18 Meadow Close
Wodley
Stockport SK6 1QZ
Tel 0161-430-6970

Cake Art Ltd
Venture Way
Crown Estate
Priorswood
Taunton TA2 8DE
Tel 01823-321532

Holly Products
Holly Cottage
Hassall Green
Sandbach
Cheshire CW11 0YA
Tel & Fax 01270-761403

Orchard Products
51 Hallyburton Road
Hove
East Sussex BN3 7GP
Tel 01273-419418
Fax 01273-412512

Sugarcraft Creations
35 Lidget Street
Lindley
Huddersfield HD3 3JB
Tel & Fax 01484-460585

J.F.Renshaw Ltd
Crown Street
Liverpool L8 7RF
Tel 0151-706-8200

James Fleming & Co Ltd
Newbridge
Midlothian
Scotland EH28 2PA
Tel 0131-333-2323
Fax 0131-333-3991

Guy Paul & Co Ltd
Unit B4
Foundry Way
Little End Road
Eaton Socon
Cambs PE19 3JH
Tel 01480-472545

Just Vena
40 Friars Avenue
Shenfield
Essex CM15 8HU
Tel 01277-234926

Kit Box templates supplied by
DRF Technical Services
1 Fernlea Gardens
Easton in Gordano
Avon BS20 0JF
Tel & Fax 01275-374557

Anniversary House
(Cake Decorations) Ltd
Unit 5
Roundways
Elliott Road
Bournemouth BH11 8JJ
Tel: 01202-590222

Squires Kitchen
Squires House
3 Waverley Lane
Farnham
Surrey GU9 8BB
Tel: 01252-711749